the JOURNEY

11/19/14

To: Norma
Fr: Joan

Thank you for sharing in my journey. You also have a story to share. Please share yours also.

Juliett

the JOURNEY
Pursuing the Path to Your Promise

Joan Whittaker

TATE PUBLISHING
AND ENTERPRISES, LLC

The Journey
Copyright © 2014 by Joan Whittaker. All rights reserved.

No part of this publication may be reproduced, stored in a retrieval system or transmitted in any way by any means, electronic, mechanical, photocopy, recording or otherwise without the prior permission of the author except as provided by USA copyright law.

Scripture quotations, unless otherwise indicated, are taken from the *Holy Bible, King James Version*, Cambridge, 1769. Used by permission. All rights reserved.

Scripture quotations marked (NKJV) are taken from the *New King James Version*. Copyright © 1982 by Thomas Nelson, Inc. Used by permission. All rights reserved.

The opinions expressed by the author are not necessarily those of Tate Publishing, LLC.

Published by Tate Publishing & Enterprises, LLC
127 E. Trade Center Terrace | Mustang, Oklahoma 73064 USA
1.888.361.9473 | www.tatepublishing.com

Tate Publishing is committed to excellence in the publishing industry. The company reflects the philosophy established by the founders, based on Psalm 68:11,
"The Lord gave the word and great was the company of those who published it."

Book design copyright © 2014 by Tate Publishing, LLC. All rights reserved.
Cover design by Junriel Boquecosa
Interior design by Caypeeline Casas

Published in the United States of America

ISBN: 978-1-62902-036-5
1. Self-Help / Personal Growth / General
2. Self-Help / Motivational & Inspirational
14.02.03

Dedication

Thanks be to God who has given me the inspiration, strength, and patience to write this book.

I dedicate this book to Mark, Bryan, and Twudian, my three children, as well as the many other children I have adopted into my life. You have all participated and shared in my journey to find my purpose in life. We have laughed and cried together and have made many stops along the way. I hope that the decisions I have made will leave a lasting legacy that you will carry on to the next generation.

To Mark. After your struggles are over, and you find your place under the stars, may you mount up with wings as an eagle. May your true kind heart and superb personality surface and impact the world for the greater good.

To Bryan. May your brilliant, creative attributes, dedication, and commitment to your ministry continue to transform lives now and until the end of time.

To my only birth daughter, Twudian. May your leadership skills, wisdom, and multitude of gifts serve our children and adults until your days on this planet are over.

Also, to the many children I have adopted, thank you for giving me the opportunity to come into your lives and to interrupt your path. May you all blossom and find your purpose because after all the problems and struggles are over, God will take you into the promise land.

Contents

Foreword 9
Introduction 11

Part 1
Let My People Go

Emancipate Yourself 17
The Red Sea Is Not a Dead End 31
When God Changes Direction 41
God Will Watch Your Back 51
Celebrate Your Victories 61

Part 2
The Wilderness

In the Wilderness with a Promise 75
Rephidim: A Place of Refreshing 89
Sinai: A Place of Intimacy with God 103
Jordan: Barrier or Opportunity 113
Jericho: Bringing Down the Walls 121

Part 3
In the Promise Land

Taking Territories 137

Managing Success... 171

Dealing with the Enemy.. 183

Leaving a Legacy of Excellence 195

Enjoy the Journey! 209

Appendix 223

About the Author 225

Notes 229

Foreword

I have known Pastor Joan Whittaker for several years in the capacity as spiritual leader and covering. I think one word that comes to mind when I think of her is fearless! In the times that I have visited her ministry or when she has visited ours, one thing that I can be sure of is that she will have something new to tell me. Whether it be a part of the vision that has come to completion or a challenge that she is facing and believing God to bring her through, I've always noted her consistency and tenacity with her walk with God. It seems only right that at this juncture in her life. She put pen to paper to give us an insight into her journey. It's a journey that we all must take, and The Journey from Pastor Whittaker's standpoint is unique and impacting. I believe every reader who takes the time to read this personal and profound literary presentation will find something to assist them on their own life's journey.

The Journey is set to the backdrop of Moses and his challenges, successes, and frustrations as a leader embarking on one of the most incredible journeys of all time. Pastor Whittaker uses the various scenarios of his life to illustrate key lessons for us to learn as we take our own personal journey of life. This together with her personal thoughts and shared chapters of her own life provide a practical guide to the reader who is willing to learn the lessons God wants to teach. The listed "Power

Points" at the conclusion of each chapter provide a constructive focus tool as you prepare to read the next. *The Journey: Pursuing the Path to Your Promise* is a book I believe we can all identify with and one I believe will be a blessing to the body of Christ.

Bishop John Francis
Ruach City Church, UK

Introduction

Enjoying God from Start to Finish

Unquestionably, life is a journey that can be enjoyed from start to finish. Life has a starting point and a destination. Birth and death provide access to enter and exit life. Despite the vicissitudes of life, the disappointments, and problems that we face, we can finish life's journey with grace. It is even more exciting to know that the believers' walk with God is also a journey. The difference is, it never ends, you simply move from one glory to another.

The journey of the Israelites from Egypt to Canaan symbolizes the journey of every person who chooses to walk with God. We have all experienced bondage, freedom, the wilderness, etc., while trying to seek Canaan. Many people abort their destiny by denying God the opportunity to move them from one phase of the journey to another. If we become convinced that God has created the same path for us with the same pattern of experiences, then our perspective regarding our life will change. We will appreciate the stops along the way rather than complain about them. I am now a half of a century old, and suddenly, my eyes are open to the revelation that all my experiences and encounters were only a part of the journey. When I was a little girl, I always dreamed of becoming someone of importance.

In fact, my late cousin George Sewell and I made a pact when we were twelve years old that we would one day attend college and become doctors. George wanted to become a medical doctor, and I wanted to become a college professor. George became a medical doctor at an early age and died an untimely death. I was compelled to carry on our dreams.

When I was four years old, my mother died dramatically while giving birth. My aunt, Granny Pin, who was a single mother, quickly became my mother. For many years, Granny Pin did the best she could to raise all of her seven children and nine others from my mother. I learned many lessons from Granny Pin, who was a mother and father to over a dozen children. I saw her tenacity, determination, and will to survive against all odds. She was a great woman of God. She did not have much, but she had a big God. I'm sure I was expected to become another statistic in our small, poor, rural town of not more than two thousand people. However, God had another plan. I was told that my mother's last prayer to God was for her baby girls to grow up and become spiritual leaders. I'm sure God gave her a promise, and he is now manifesting it through my ministry. I have few memories of my mother. Yet I remember her funeral like it was yesterday. Thousands of people, young and old, spent days mourning, singing, and expressing their grief. God must have protected me from the deep agony that others could not bear for a reason. I have longed to know my mother. However, I never missed a mother figure because Granny Pin and my grandmother filled the gap.

My father was a remarkable business man, organizer, and committed worker despite him being illiterate. I remember penning his letters to others and reading them aloud. I always read those letters painfully. I was motivated with my own dreams and vowed that I would never find myself in my father's position educationally. My eyes were opened to the fact that even with handicaps and deficiencies, God can use anyone. The few years I spent living close to my father, I learned that he was a great preacher, servant leader, and a man of God who made an impact on many lives. My father decided to remarry and move away from our town when I was only twelve years old. My older sister and I were left to be raised solely by our Granny Pin.

Today, I am a senior pastor and library director. On the journey, I experienced: marriage, childbirth, divorce, pain, joy, immigration, relocation, living single, successes, failures, and all the things that happen along the way. Against all odds, I have made it and count it all joy. Many Christians miss the basic principle in the Word of God that while there is an Egypt, there is also a promise land. Moreover, while there is a wilderness, there is also a place of plenty. There is a path to the destination that everyone must follow. Along the way, there will be stops, mountains, valleys, rivers to cross, and a multitude of encounters. However, none of these things are meant to destroy us but rather to perfect us.

Wherever you are on the journey, go through it because it will not last. I find that when you know where you are going and you are equipped with the necessary tools, you will not be deterred. Your destination, as it was for the children of Israel, must be the promise land. You must remain focused on your dream, as well as the personal promises that God has made to you in order to bring you into a place of plenty. The general and specific promises that God has made to you are meant to bring you successfully to your destination. Your destination counts. You must focus on where you are headed, and you will not be sidetracked. You must have a target, a dream, something to keep your perspective right when life gets challenging. The great Apostle Paul describes life as a race with a destination and a point of beginning. We must run slowly because the race is not for the swift but for those who endure to the end. Where we are now must be understood as a stop, an experience, or an encounter that is only temporary. We should remain focused on the prize while we enjoy the many occurrences along the way. The goal of this book is to transform the thinking of the reader, to understand that life is a journey. The chapters in this book will parallel our lives. Finally, I want readers to understand that our walk with God is a journey. God takes us from one point to another to enrich our lives with his blessings. As the wind of change moves us from one point to another, we must understand that if our steps are ordered by the Almighty God, then it will be well. There are no exceptions to this rule.

PART 1

LET MY PEOPLE GO

Emancipate Yourself

> Come now therefore, and I will send thee unto Pharaoh that thou mayest bring forth my people the children of Israel out of Egypt.
>
> Exodus 3:10 (KJV)

God desires to free everyone from the bondage that sin creates in our lives. It was never God's intention to watch man live each day in servitude. God created Adam and Eve and gave them freedom. He gave them the ability to make choices. God has also given us the power of choice. Our choices impact lives for good or evil. Our choices may open doors to great opportunities and bring success or failure. Our choices may result in sleepless nights or abundant joy. The choices we make may send us on a tidal wave of consequences. Some of our choices have left us scarred for life. Adam and Eve blew the greatest opportunity anyone could have. Today, millions of people live under the taskmaster of sin, through drugs, alcohol, sexual immorality, religious philosophy, and abuse of all kinds. However, they don't understand that God has a better way and a plan for their lives. God is ready, willing, and able to liberate anyone and everyone from the strongholds of sin. We now have an opportunity to liberate ourselves from the pain and disappointments of the past and to live in freedom in Christ. It is possible to wake up every day and enjoy life. Your current circumstance does not have to determine your attitude. I have chosen today to have life and to enjoy it. I know there is a God who has made a promise to me that he would keep me in perfect peace.

Many years ago, I was studying at the University of the West Indies. I majored in West Indian history. The history of the West Indian people, in essence, is a history of the institution of slavery and its aftermath. I was asked quite frequently in my course work to analyze the factors that contributed to the abolition of slavery. Slavery was barbaric and was meant to break a person's will to live. There were no opportunities to explore personal goals or dreams. However, as I searched for the reasons why the institution could not work forever, I found that each human being was created with an innate desire for freedom. The absenteeism of plantation owners, sympathizers who helped, and the stand of abolitionist all played key roles in the abolition of slavery. However, I found that the driving force to be free within the slaves was the most potent weapon they had in their arsenal. Human beings were not created to be slaves. They were born to be free. Through rebellion, many slaves began to show their discontent and disapproval of the institution. Leaders were birthed out of the roots of slavery. They were prepared to give their lives for the cause of freedom. Despite the high risk factor, rebellions, riots, and runaways were the norm on many plantations because of the desire for freedom.

> And Afterward Moses and Aaron went in, and told Pharaoh, Thus saith the Lord God of

Israel. Let my people go, that they may hold a feast unto me in the wilderness.

Exodus 5:1 (KJV)

A personal passion and desire to be free will create opportunities for freedom. Moses was called out by God to become a liberator. His leadership would exemplify one of the greatest emancipation initiatives on the planet. The Israelites in Egypt wanted freedom. After four hundred years, they decided that enough was enough! The children of Israel heard of talks concerning their father Abraham and the life of freedom during the time of Joseph. They were determined that their current situation would not last. Their cries were heard by God. God remembered his promise to Abraham. Abraham's descendants were to be as the number of the sand of the sea. God also promised Abraham a land flowing with milk and honey. God promised the children of Israel prosperity and freedom. A significant amount of time had lapsed between the promise God made to Abraham and the Egyptian slavery experience. However, God's word and promises supersede time and space. The moment God brings his word to pass is greater than the time we wait on him. Through the death, burial, and resurrection of Jesus Christ, God has provided everyone with the opportunity to be adopted into his family. God's plan for our lives as his children is for us to be free to live every day joyfully. The decision for freedom is ours. God wants to emancipate and liberate us. His destiny is for us to take the journey from Egypt to the promise land. Make a decision now to begin the journey. God has designed every stop, encounter, and/or experience to bring you into your destiny.

Pharaoh Can't Stop You

Pharaoh realized that he had lost free labor and the power of control. After releasing the Israelites, also called Hebrews, he pursued them. God, the deliverer, was prepared for this. God knew that Pharaoh, symbolically Satan, would revisit those whom God delivered. Satan's desire is to destroy the soul of man, and he does so in a very attractive way. He entices, offers gifts, and provides pleasure. However, his gifts come with a great price. His scheme is to bring you back into slavery. Yet greater is he who is in you than he who is in the world. I remember vividly the day I accepted Jesus into my heart as my savior. I attended a little country church called the Church of God of Prophecy. I was at the tender age of fourteen, and I was in a physical and emotional transition period from a little girl to an adolescent. I experienced the power of forgiveness. I literally wept for hours at the altar. I asked God to forgive me of my sins even though I could not recall most of them. I also remember the night when I was baptized with the Holy Spirit. The spiritual mothers who stood around me prophetically declared that I had received many spiritual gifts from the Lord.

At that time, I did not understand anything concerning spiritual gifts or the destiny that God designed for me. The enemy evidently understood what took place because he certainly pursued me during my teenage years. Looking back, I understand clearly the plan the enemy had for me. He was after the promises God made to me. He intended to destroy my life because of what he knew would occur in the future. At age eighteen, I married a man who was not saved. He had a job, a nice car, and knew how to sweet talk anyone. I was head over heels in love with him. After two months into the marriage, I knew that I had made a grave mistake. After several years of running from God, I returned to God in a state of embarrassment. I was lonely, deprived of affection, as well as mentally and emotionally drained. My personal world had fallen apart, and I reached for God with everything in my being. I needed help, fast. There were no relatives, friends, or colleagues who could help to remove the pain I felt each day. I felt rejected, disappointed, and self-hatred for being ignorant on how to make better choices. I have personally received deliverance over and over during times of trouble because of my attitude toward God. I recall during this time that someone informed me that my husband said that he was not returning home. I found myself in the middle of a separation in my marriage. Despite my emotional pain, in my response was a determination to continue to praise God with more fervor. I know that many people observing my praise during church services were puzzled because they knew my private issues. However, deep down in my spirit, I felt like a conqueror because I developed an attitude of praise and thanksgiving. I believe that I was able to make it during this difficult time because of my habit of praising God every day. I did not fall into deep depression. I, however, was able to encourage the children, continue to work to maintain my family, and grow as never before in my walk with God.

However, God rescued me from the hands of Pharaoh—the devil, the deceiver. He gave me a second chance. I took responsibility for the choices I made. I have never lived my life blaming others for the bad choices I made. My world was self-created. I remained married for many years, and my pain was intensified every year. Yet God drew me closer to him and taught me how to rejoice in the midst of the pain. The journey had just begun. I was emancipated from Egypt. The burden of the taskmaster was no longer my daily experience. I was being trained to trust God in the midst of adversity. I could not be stopped. The mistake the devil made was to allow me to leave Egypt.

Similarly, you must believe in yourself and the fact that God has a plan for your life and will never leave you to manage your situations and circumstances without support. God has a tremendous support system that is guaranteed to keep you in any circumstance. Now, I frequently counsel people who are going through the same experiences I encountered and to some extent, some of which I am still going through. Yet I find those who rise above the pain to succeed and mature are those who have changed their perspective regarding their situation. Most problems are temporary and may not necessarily go away or be solved completely. The ability of the individual to deal with the issues at hand in a positive way determines successful outcomes. Our perspective is critical to the outcome. Our outlook must be positive at all times, even when there appears to be no answer in sight. I have seen problems get solved after refusing to give too much attention to emergent situations. Do not become absorbed in the mistakes of the past. Everyone makes mistakes, especially when we are at a place of immaturity and living a life with no real accountability. Many of us, for one reason or another, have not had the freedom to make the right choices. For a multitude of reasons, we make mistakes and end up in places that we did not bargain for nor plan for. However, the paramount idea is that we do not judge ourselves from the past but pick up the pieces from where we are now and move on. We always have today to work with. There is no situation that is beyond fixing. There is no life that is beyond repair. There is no one that cannot change their life, attitude, and behavior. As long as we are alive, we can make changes to our lives.

If you are in the physical prison, serving time, you can be just as free as the person who walks the street every day because freedom is a mental condition. We must become radical in our thinking. For example, I refuse to let anyone or anything judge me today based on my past immature decisions. I have made a decision to take control of my life and plan my future based on the purpose that God has designed for my life. We must know who we are and the incredible gifts we have built in our personalities to succeed. Slavery is a state of mind. Unfortunately, for the Hebrews, they were delivered from slavery but continued to live within the confines of the same state of mind. It is better to have just a little with freedom rather than to have much without the ability to live free. We must not allow our negative experiences to have power over us and dictate how we lead our lives. Once you are free, just put one foot forward every day and keep moving. Begin with baby steps if you must but just keep moving. Endeavor to move from point A to point B. Complacency will rob you of your right to get to your destination. You have a right to your future, and you have one opportunity to live life to the fullest. All of us at some point in our lives have made decisions that have led us into places of bondage. Yet, the beauty is all of us have the opportunity to pick up the pieces and start over. Don't miss your opportunity to begin again. Don't miss your second chance.

We may ask, "How do I start over?" Look around you; people are placed in your life for a reason. Find a mentor, a coach, or just ask people who are older and more experienced on how they made it. Words of encouragement from my colleagues, pastor, friend, mentor, etc., have served to motivate me to get up and begin. The Bible is loaded with a wealth of information and life-giving encouragement on how to achieve. Books are essential to learning, as well as to spiritual and emotional and psychological development. Develop a prayer life and meditate on the Word of God, and resolve every day that today will be better than yesterday and that tomorrow will be better than today. People who are born to be great oftentimes experience a greater level of challenge in their lives. Passing the tests that life presents moves us one stage at a time, from maturity to maturity. We will never be given great life responsibilities until we have proven that we have the integrity to manage the responsibility. Smart people know that success comes after hard work and many trials and sacrifices. The things that seem to come to destroy you, don't rebuke them but seek to learn from them. Hidden in your problems are the greatest opportunities for success. There is no new trick from Satan because he lacks creativity. The cycle of negatives that is presented is always the same for all of us. God, however, is creative and has a variety of solutions to any one problem. The secret is to seek godly guidance as you move forward. Take charge of your destiny today by submitting to the one who has the authority and power to guide your life until you get to your place of promise. Some days, you may feel like returning to past negative practices because it's easier to do that, but let us all take the high road. The path of the high road may sometimes be more challenging, but ultimately, the results will be beneficial rather than detrimental.

Don't Go Back, Don't Look Back

> Being confident of this very thing, that He which has begun a good work in you will perform it until the day of Jesus Christ.
>
> Philippians 1:6 (KJV)

Throughout history, countless people have turned from a life of sin to a life of righteousness orchestrated by God. The problem is that as a pig returns to its wallow, many people return to the very thing they were delivered from. This is a travesty because Jesus emphasized that the last state of that man will be worse than the first. The children of Israel were classic complainers, frequently worrying about their current situation. They refused, early in the journey, to give God a chance to prove himself. They refused to allow their faith to work. The Israelites were not out of Egypt good and swiftly began to demonstrate a spirit of ingratitude. They quickly forgot the many miracles and signs that were wrought by the hands of God on their behalf. In the initial stages of the journey, the new believer cannot follow the children of Israel's example. The new believer must express gratitude and appreciation for the grace that God has extended. A lifestyle of gratefulness has to be developed instead of a life of complaining. Giving God thanks for everything must become a daily habit. The Israelites were surrounded by recent memories of the benefits of slavery. Yet they could have easily maintained focus on where they were going by trusting God.

God demonstrated that he was able to create miracles on many occasions. However, memories of the smell of food in Egypt, the comfort of its houses, and the luxury of a host of other material possessions captivated their imaginations. They forgot that they were no longer in slavery. The devil will quickly compare your current situation, particularly the negative, to the accounts of the past. Every effort must be made to keep focused by looking steadfastly to the future. A God-motivated individual will learn to keep moving, trusting, anticipating, and believing, even when reality speaks otherwise. A forward-thinking individual will maintain perspective, even during the roughest times. He or she understands that a storm is temporary and must pass. It is a tool that must be used to maintain peace of mind. My favorite scripture during tough times is Philippians 1:6, being confident of the work God has started and his ability to complete it. This scripture is paramount to the success of a child of God in moving into his or her destiny. Confidence is believing in what you do and why you do what you do, even if no one else believes in you. Confidence is maintaining a positive attitude that is not swayed by a change in the climate of things around you.

Recently, as the executive director of a library, I was faced with an unexpected budget cut at the end of the fiscal year. I was trained not to panic but to search for solutions to address this fiscal crisis. I was determined not to be discouraged. I was determined to weather this storm and claim the victory. I presented the situation to God in prayer and asked for a strategy. God gave me the solution to address the situation. Respect, truth, and confidence were employed during the negotiations, and the funds were restored. My point is that God has a stored basket of solutions awaiting every believer. The same resources are available to the experienced Christian, as well as the new believer. God will provide every tool that is needed to be successful and to overcome the devices of the enemy during the journey. The good work that God has started will be completed. God is not a man that he should lie or the son of man that he should repent from his word. What a consolation to know that God does not repent. His word is solid like a rock. His word is consistent. His word is true and will never fail.

Most of the prophecies that were spoken over my life at age fourteen have materialized. There are only a few prophecies that are yet to manifest. My destiny was planned before the foundations of the world. Moreover, God has planned your destiny before the journey actually began. There is no stopping now. God desires to move you from Egypt to the next stage of the journey. You cannot afford to look back spiritually, mentally, or emotionally because the moment you change your focus, your hard work will be wasted. People get stuck in the past because they fail to believe that they have the power to break negative cycles. Against all odds, we can make it because success, as we will see later, is oftentimes defined by material possession. Success must be seen also as the ability to weather storms along the way and accomplish our life dreams despite them. Life is like a project. Every project must be addressed according to its stage of development. During the first stage, the initiation period, missions, visions, and plans are birthed. Next, during the coordination phase, resources are solicited and gathered. Then there is the stage of implementation when the plan is executed. The final stage, in general terms, is the stage of assessment when outcomes are measured. Our lives are like a project that must be developed one phase at a time or one season at a time. We must know which phase we are living in. Questions must be asked. Am I at the stage of initiation wherein I am still developing my personal goals and objectives, or am I at the point where I am implementing my plans? Let's be reminded that the journey comes in phases, seasons, or sections. We must pay particular attention to the point where we are in the journey. Those who attempt to begin at the destination will never be able to carry the responsibility and weight that comes with that phase. It's important to note that we are a work in progress. We are constantly being refashioned and remade into better vessels as we mature in our relationships with God and man.

We are carriers of great treasures, and interestingly, the treasures we carry must be released in the form of our contributions to the development of other lives before we leave this earth. It is very possible for anyone from any background to rise above the negatives, become accomplished, and later leave deposits of themselves in a positive way in the lives of those they encounter. There is a good work that has been placed in all human beings that must be watered, nourished, and protected, and bear fruit. We were born to be offered to the world after the good work comes to maturity. Cooperation on our part is required if we are going to be perfected to be offered to the world. Imperfections are demonstrated in the lack of integrity we see around us, in individuals who are labeled as professionals and role models. No one will ever be perfect, but a basic requirement of good conduct must be maintained. Cooperation means submitting in obedience to those who are placed as leaders over us in order for our character to be developed. There are times when we may be embarrassed and/or disappointed in the process, but the right attitude must be maintained at all times. It is impossible for us to see everything from the perspective of those who lead because the visionary sees the future, while we tend to see the present in our roles as subordinates. It is therefore imperative that we trust the master of our lives and give him the permission to guide us. At the beginning of the journey, we are diamonds in the rough, waiting to be processed for the day when we will shine. In time, we will shine as long as we don't go back and don't look back.

Power Points of This Chapter

- Sin is connected to bondage.
- God desires for everyone to be free from the bondage that sin creates.
- We have the power to make choices. The choices we make will either bring us into bondage or into freedom.
- We have to create a lifestyle that is developed in gratitude and not complaint.
- We must realize that storms don't last forever. Once we realize that our storms are on a time limit, we can have peace of mind, God's peace.
- Remain focused; don't look back because you were born to be offered to the world.

The Red Sea Is Not a Dead End

> My brothers, I do not count myself to have taken possession, but one thing I do, forgetting the things behind and reaching forward to the things before, I press toward the mark for the prize of the high calling of God in Christ Jesus.
>
> Philippians 3:13 (NKJV)

Reconcile with the Past: Untie, Loose, Undo

Recently, I taught a lesson on the power of forgiveness. I underscored the consequences of holding on to past pain, baggage, hurt feelings, and old relationships. I shared the story of a young Christian woman. Her best friend seduced, slept with, and stole her husband. Soon after, the woman's husband divorced her and married the friend. She inhaled pain and exhaled bitterness. She slept every night with anger, rejection, and low self-esteem while constantly seeing the face of the other woman in her mind's eye. After years of hating her "friend turned foe," she visited a conference. The session she attended focused on the power of forgiveness. She was taught that only through the power of Christ's blood can one obtain the ability to forgive. She learned that Jesus utilized love on the cross to conquer the pain of unforgiveness. She listened intently to the description of the life of a person driven by the stronghold of bitterness and resentment. Every participant was asked to pray. The leaders of the session also prayed that the Holy Spirit would enter the hearts of each participant and work on them. A river of love filled the heart of the young woman, and she was set free. On her way home, she called her old best friend. She met with her and resolved the past. Only then was she able to move on and accomplish great things. She could not change what happened, but she could change where she was going. Disconnection from the strongholds of the past must take place in order for anyone to move on to a new beginning. One of the greatest entrapments to anyone's progress is to retain old memories, old ways of thinking, philosophies, and opinions. A process of untying, undoing, and loosing must take place in order to be liberated emotionally and psychologically.

Jesus encountered a woman who lived a lifestyle of prostitution. She came running to him because of the genuine love she felt emanating from him. She was also drawn to the Lord because she felt his comfort would overshadow her rejection and pain. Jesus didn't embarrass her. He responded, "Woman thou art loosed from thine infirmities." Jesus loosed her from the stronghold of the past. God desires to loose you from the stronghold of your past as well. God's love and mercy is able to set anyone free from the bondage of slavery. God is equally able to keep those whom he sets free. Countless people share their testimonies of the delivering power of God every day. Yet we must make daily and consistent efforts to free ourselves. Two of the greatest tools of liberation are to learn to love yourself and see yourself as God sees you. Our greatest critic and judge can sometimes be our personal demons who tell us we are not forgiven. Someone asked me, "How could God love me? I am all messed up and don't deserve God's love because of all the things I have done." My response was, "That is exactly why Jesus Christ died, to love and forgive us nevertheless."

Like the woman earlier who had to forgive to disconnect, so must we forgive in order to untie, loose, and undo ourselves from the chains that connect us to the past. Can you see now that even though the children of Israel were physically out of Egypt, they were still enslaved mentally? That's why they were miserable, disobedient, discontented, and unable to see beyond their situation. They were blinded by the baggage of slavery. They were liberated but were still thinking and acting like slaves. They yearned for slave food, slave clothing, slave houses, and everything they had before. God had an awesome future prepared for them. If only they could see that and become excited about the adventure awaiting them. Endless possibilities, opportunities, and encounters are awaiting us. God is waiting to explore with us as he teaches us. Hold on and enjoy the ride!

We cannot allow ourselves to be trapped by our past experiences. Many of us today are still living in our past. I frequently encounter people who are not delivered from the pain of incidences which occurred years ago. Consequently, they live with rejection, bitterness, low self-esteem, and an array of emotions that control their lives. Even when they find true love, they are not able to appreciate the new things and new people in their lives, who genuinely care. So life becomes a cycle of moving from one broken relationship to another. These people, generally, are not successful at their goals and objectives because their greatest enemies are not other people but themselves. It's that enemy inside of us that, if allowed to prevail, will abort our destiny. Everyone walks around with a certain demeanor that either attracts or repels the good. Many of us repel great opportunities to move us into a great future. It is critical that we believe in ourselves more than any other person. But we may ask, "How do I get free from this horrible thing that he/she did to me?" My freedom from the past came from my acceptance of who I am in Christ. I woke up one day and realized that I was made to love because I have a God who loves me. God thinks good thoughts about me and has a great plan for my life. We must all come to the realization that we are loved by God. This truth provides me with the weapon to love myself in a healthy way and love others as a result. I now dream big, make big sacrifices to accomplish my dreams, and wake up each day knowing that I am no longer trapped by my circumstances. I am free to make the best choices for my life. Who has made me free? The credit goes to God first, then my sheer willingness to look beyond my negative feelings and move on with my life. I did not wait for someone to come along and love me out of my pain. I did not blame anyone for my mistakes. I took responsibility for my life and decided that I will not blow this one opportunity. No one and nothing will rob me of my God-given right to accomplish my dreams.

The Red Sea Is Not a Barrier

Poised on the brink of the Red Sea, the children of Israel were scared, confused, and apprehensive. They thought that Moses was only a man and that he did not have the capability or the resources to get them across. There were no boats in sight. They began to focus on the enemy in fast pursuit and the waves in front of them. They were lacking faith. Faith is trusting God when there are no resources available to solve the problem. God positions all of us on the brink of our breakthrough. He watches us to see if we will make the choice to depend on him or succumb to doubt and fear. I believe God deliberately allows us to face the waters of the Red Sea to prove to us that he is capable and in charge. The Red Sea is not a barrier. God does not create barriers to our success but opportunities through personal encounters with him. If we look at the waters with the natural eye, it will lead us to believe that we're headed for destruction. Yet the waters we face are meant to perfect us. Many doors are invisible to the naked eye, but they generally take on the appearance of the structure. However, God has a door ready to open right in the midst of the turbulent waters of life. God promises that he will always make a way of escape so that we will be able to bear it. In other words, God will never give his people more than we can bear.

It is significant to take note of the response of the people to the Red Sea. They lost all memory of the previous miracles wrought by the hands of God through Moses. They were completely focused on the crisis at hand. They were absorbed mentally, emotionally, and psychologically. The enemy will always come running after us in order to drain us of our peace and mental stamina. The devil's desire is to move quickly and swiftly with great commotion. Yet at the last moment, God shows up with a mighty breakthrough. The mighty waters of the Red Sea were opened by God. The door to the greatest opportunity in the life of the Israelites was flung open. At the same time, the enemies in pursuit were destroyed in the same waters that saved lives. What God uses to deliver you will be the same thing that will be used to destroy your enemies. Remember the problem that was meant to kill you; God used it as a stepping-stone to launch you to the next level. God has the ability to manipulate situations and circumstances to bring to pass anything he desires. Do you see that all Jehovah God was doing was to introduce himself in a better way to the Israelites? God creatively and brilliantly utilizes detrimental situations to bring us closer to him. As we move closer to him in obedience and full trust, God unfolds himself in a new way. God is waiting to open another door of opportunity, but we must be positioned in the right place at the right time. It is vital to understand that God also introduces people into our lives to help open doors. Several years ago, one of the greatest miracles in my life occurred. God told me to resign as a pastor from the church organization, which I was a member of for approximately fifteen years. The decision to walk away from the fellowship with the people I love and respect was excruciatingly painful. More pain was inevitable because I knew that they would not understand that God wanted something else for me and obviously had other plans. I was distraught emotionally. The human side of me was apprehensive. The spiritual side said, "It's a God move." After six months of indecision, despite the fact that the church I pastored gave their full support, encouragement, and confirmation, I made the move. I was scared, but I faced my fears and resigned. Shortly after my resignation, I went into serious depression, mixed with the ingredients of emotional and spiritual chaos. I separated myself from everyone. I sought the face of God for forty days in deep fasting and prayer. At the end of my consecration, I heard a small voice saying, "Go to England." I knew it was the voice of God. I obeyed, purchased my ticket, and took the bold risk without knowing what I would be faced with. This one bold step of faith opened a new world for me. I was challenged, motivated, and excited at the end of my short, one-week trip. God divinely connected me with my spiritual father. My obedience was a bridge to my miracle. I met my current Bishop who said one phrase that transformed my life. He said, "Think big!" I thought to myself, *Me, a woman, single, divorced, crushed over and over by people around me, pastoring a small church with no great aspirations to grow beyond one hundred members was told to think big.* This one moment in time changed my life. I was now, for the first time, liberated to pursue my dreams within the confines of God's will for my life. I had crossed over the Red Sea and was ready for an exciting new journey with God.

Faith Opens Doors

The group of Hebrews that journeyed from Egypt consisted of all types of personalities. Later in this book, we will see that they developed a camp mentality rather than focusing on the God-given vision ahead. From the outset, it was evident that they were doubters, quite similar to many of us today who do not practice what we preach. Faith is elusive for many of us. It is a subject that is thoroughly taught and explored by scholars, novices, mature believers, as well as anyone from anywhere. Faith, however, continues to be a challenge because it is easy to speak on the subject but challenging to live and practice. There are levels of faith, ranging from the faith that is required by all persons who accept Jesus Christ as their Lord to the more mature faith described by St. Paul nearing the end of his journey. Abraham, the Father of the Hebrew nation, for instance, exercised mature faith when he died believing God without witnessing the realization of some of the promises God made to him. The Bible defines faith in Hebrews 11:1: "Now faith is the substance of things hoped for the evidence of things not seen" (KJV). Faith, then, is inextricably tied to the word of God and is paramount to spiritual success. It has the ability to create paths out of seemingly huge impossible things like the Red Sea. Let's take the word "substance" from the scripture given. It means confident, and confidence is derived from the Greek word "hupostasis." On exploring the meaning of the word "substance" further, it means that which is placed under, foundation, support, or reality.

Faith can be properly defined then as that which gives reality or substance to things hoped for. Faith, for us, then must be equal to our reality. I must see it, claim it, believe it, live it, act it, etc. Faith must become the very foundation on which we stand every day. Unfortunately, most of us are very reactive in terms of the way we live our lives. Rather than taking charge by being proactive, we react in doubt and fear based on what we see confronting us. Moses was admonished by God to lift up the rod he carried, stretch it over the sea, and divide the waters. God was saying to Moses, "You do have the resource and the weapon necessary to deal with this crisis. It's right in your hand. It may not look like a weapon, but yes, if you make the move of faith, you will see results." Moses led brilliantly as he remained calm in the midst of a great crisis with a multitude of nervous and apprehensive people applying great pressure for him to resolve the situation on hand. He consulted God as any good leader would do, reassured the people, maintained his poise, and responded with confidence. Where there is faith, there is no fear. Faith removes the spirit of fear and helps us to see clearly. It is imperative that we learn the value of faith in the beginning of the journey because it is impossible for us to get to our destination without this important tool.

    I have countless testimonies of faith at work in my life. I recall during the purchase of our first church facility I was given the arduous task of locating a mortgage for the purchase. After being rejected by about fifteen banks consecutively, I was asked one day by the mortgage broker, "Do you really believe that God told you to make this purchase? Should I move on to look for other properties? Nothing appears to be working out." I paused to gather my composure over the phone because I could feel the spirit of fear saying, "Yes, believe her, and end the deal on the table." Seconds felt like hours as I mentally played out all the hard work that went into the project, and most importantly, I remembered when God said to call that number listed on the property. After the long pause, I responded quietly but confidently. "Yes, this is the property." Within a couple months from that step of faith, we received a mortgage.

Power Points of This Chapter

- Two of the greatest tools of liberation are to learn to love yourself and see yourself as God sees you.
- What God uses to deliver you will be the same thing that will be used to destroy your enemies.
- The problem that was meant to kill you, God used it as a stepping-stone to launch you to the next level.
- God creatively and brilliantly utilizes detrimental situations to bring us closer to him.
- Faith is trusting God when there are no resources available to solve the problem.
- God positions all of us on the brink of our breakthrough

When God Changes Direction

> And Jehovah spoke to Moses saying, Speak to the sons of Israel that they turn and camp before Pihahiroth, between Migdol and the sea, over against Baal-sephon. You shall camp before it, by the sea.
>
> Exodus 14:2 (NKJV)

The children of Israel were headed north, the most popular and well-known route to Canaan. God watched them for a while and then said to Moses, "Turn around. I want you to go southeast." God changed direction on them and sent them right on the brink of the mighty sea. Lessons of obedience must be taught to everyone who desires great things in God. God wanted his people to follow his direction, not their own. We can speculate and attempt to dissect the thoughts of God as to why he wanted them to take this route. Yet the bottom line is God was simply testing their level of obedience. It is easy for us to seek our own path and plot our own course. However, I believe God wants to challenge us. In God's challenge, we will learn, grow, and mature spiritually, mentally, and emotionally. The worst location was chosen. Who would desire to be placed between their enemy and a raging ocean, especially when you cannot swim? The world calls it "between a rock and a hard place." Have you been ever placed between a rock and a hard place? Either way will be to your detriment. Human beings like to have options. We desire to see the choices that will give life and not death, the choices that will usher in abundance and not lack. As a leader, I love options. I am the type of person who looks for solutions through options; no options, no solution. But even when there are no options, God can create them. It is when you are between a rock and a hard place that God can prove himself to you. God wanted to prove himself to the children of Israel, but all they could focus on were memories of Egypt. Every mountain and monument looked like Egypt. The enemy is a master at reminding people of their past. Everything that God has delivered you from, the enemy occasionally brings them back to your attention. He amplifies every negative thought and experience, particularly when you are on the brink of your breakthrough. God will send you to camp right in front of Pihahiroth, Migdol, and Baal-zephon so that he can show you his glory. These three names carry only Egyptian connotations. Yet as Dr. Miles Monroe said in his book *The Glory of Living*, "when we experience God's omnipresence, we know His existence; when we experience God's manifest presence, we know His holiness, and when we experience God's glory, we know His power." God is waiting to reveal himself to us every day, both in the small and great things. We must be ready and prepared to be positioned by God in the midst of our rock and hard place. God's positioning always appears to be the worst. Yet hold on to your faith because your breakthrough is guaranteed!

Life Is About Managing Change

Seven years ago, as the director of a library, I sensed that it was time to change from a manual system of conducting business to a more technologically oriented way. Some progress was made in automating the majority of our systems. However, I proceeded to build a technology lab in order to provide free internet access and computer training to the underprivileged. Immediately, I was faced with the challenge of convincing everyone of the need for change. It was difficult. Reinventing yourself is one thing, but reinventing an organization is an entirely different dynamic. Great leadership skills must be employed to gain the support of all levels of staff. I sold the idea effectively to key employees. Yet there were some who had difficulty accepting that things around them were going to be different. On the opening of the technology lab, one veteran employee decided to retire because she could not handle the expectations of change. She literally cried on the shoulders of other employees and complained that she could not handle this new way of doing business. We, nevertheless, proceeded to provide these invaluable services to the community. Today, all of the changes have become the norm.

Taken completely off guard when things happen unexpectedly can sometimes be terrifying, but we must be prepared to adjust. Embracing change rather than resisting it will move us one rung higher on the ladder of life. Doors can only be opened if we are mentally prepared to walk through them. Wanting exciting things to happen but unwilling to take the plunge will not serve to move you into maturity. In my role as a pastor, one of the greatest challenges I face is to convince people that it is okay to change. Many churches hang on to old methods and old ways of delivering the gospel. They have successfully managed to turn habits into a permanent way of doing business. In fact, it is very frequent that we see man-made rules employed to supersede the principles laid down in the Word of God. Jesus Christ dealt with this problem often when he encountered the traditional system of the Pharisees. Old tools and ideas were still being used, but they were completely ineffective. We are now faced with a new generation of people whose ethos is locked into thinking, acting, and dressing completely different from the way we did ten years ago. How can we reach them? We must create dialogue, engage them, and involve them in order to harness and utilize their creativity, way of thinking, and habits. Rather than becoming judgmental, we can see the best in the worse and create a new generation that will respect the past but embrace the future. Together, old and new can cooperatively work together to move our communities into a better place. As we journey together, we can work respectfully by appreciating the gifting we collectively bring to the table. We can utilize and merge the strengths of every generation for the greater good. Life changes, and we must rise to the occasion and change ourselves. God is always doing something new, exciting, and fresh every day. God changes his methods, not his nature.

Be ready for the day when God will tell you to change your direction.

The greatest change agent the world has ever experienced was Jesus of Nazareth. He had humble beginnings, but he was born for a purpose. He was focused on his mission and was never deviated from his difficult assignment. He went about his father's business, and whenever and wherever he was rejected because he challenged the status quo, he simply moved on to continue where he left off. He was confident. He carried a level of authority that was unusual, and consequently, he was either loved or hated. Frequently, Jesus was misunderstood, doubted by the Pharisees, Sadducees, and scribes, but he kept preaching and teaching. Every change agent is faced with a certain degree of discomfort and pain. They oftentimes endure great hardship, even death, before they are able to see the fruit of their labor. Some of us are born to make greater level of sacrifices than others. Everyone is born to positively impact our world, but some of us are born to lay down our very lives in order for wrong to be made right and injustices to be eliminated. Today, Jesus is still controversial. His doctrines are embraced by millions, yet abhorred by countless people. His greatest contributions to mankind were manifested after his death, not prior to his experience on the cross. He was a change agent in life and death.

Take the Risk

Recently, my colleague in ministry and I undertook an almost impossible venture to purchase a multimillion-dollar facility labeled as a historic building in my town. This multistory structure is one of the largest buildings in the community and is listed on the tax roll as contributing significantly to the income of the municipality. This facility was the perfect building for God's vision for our church. Our church membership count was approximately two hundred people. We had little financial resources, and we knew that we were not qualified to purchase the property. Making the deal happen took every leadership skill we garnered throughout the years. We negotiated and renegotiated as one deal after another failed. Each bank we approached took us through the process of underwriting and then responded with a resounding no. Each time a deal failed, we encouraged ourselves and refused to take no for an answer. There were times when I cried and prayed. There were times I became so distraught and frustrated that I was unable to pray. However, I never lost hope. There is no failure in God. After twenty banks said no, fifteen months passed, and fourteen deals failed, we closed on the building. I learned many lessons along the way, and everyone involved came out stronger and even more determined. Truth, integrity, determination, tenacity, and doing the right thing will enable and empower you to win in the long run. Many times I was tempted to manipulate the facts, given opportunities to change information to make it happen. However, I never succumbed to the enemy. You do not have to compromise to win. God owns the cattle on a thousand hills, and all that sits on the planet belongs to him.

Risk is exposure to the possibility of loss or danger in various capacities, such as financial risk or health risk. It requires a certain level of sacrifice or investment, and the results may be detrimental rather than beneficial. The challenge is that in order to gain anything of significance in life, risk must be taken. Oftentimes, great results require a greater level of risk. Most of us do not want to give up to gain because that initial investment of time, money, and giving up the familiar for the unfamiliar can create insurmountable discomfort emotionally and psychologically. Notice the Hebrews were prepared to face the unknown as they made the decision to leave Egypt. If that decision, the risk, was not made to take the journey, they would never have inherited their place of promise. It was the risk that started and ended the journey. I was told once by my professional mentor, an older, wiser lady, that what I lacked during a crisis was the courage to terminate a member of staff. I knew it was the right thing to do, but I lacked the courage to face my fears. Risk taking is the ability to face your fears, push beyond the emotional discomfort, and begin. In my state of apprehension about going back to school to complete my doctorate degree, a colleague of mine encouraged me by stating, "I know you can do it, just begin." I took her advice and took that leap of faith. Today, looking back, I am glad I took the risk.

It's Okay to Be Different

Your path is unique because you are unique. God made you from a mold that is like no other. Some leaders expect that everyone they lead should be exactly like them. However, God loves diversity. He has created a world that is colorful with seasons that change, weather patterns that change, different food, cultures, languages, and the like. Thus, those who we lead can share our vision while maintaining their unique personalities. Everyone has qualities and gifts that can be utilized. That is why leaders should function as coverings, not lids. God does not want clones. He wants us to complement each other, respect and understand each other while not compromising our value systems. These are keys to growth and success. If we were to revisit the children of Israel, we would notice that Israel was in Egypt, but they maintained their identity as a unique race of people. They were living with the slave master who, I am sure, did everything to erase their culture and religion. However, they never compromised or forgot their history. Satan wants every memory of our relationship with God to be erased so he can fill us with his desires. He wants to replace a godly lifestyle with that of his own. Do you see that the intent is to get us to accept bondage as our norm in order to keep us enslaved? But thanks be to God, who has liberated us to think independently of the influences of the world and its philosophies. Contrary to popular belief, God does not control your personality, thoughts, emotions, ideas, etc. Rather, with our permission, God helps us to bring out the very best we have on the inside. That's why God's kingdom should be explored; because he is a God of excellence and wants to help you to become the best. The road to maturity is punctuated with challenges that are born out of our interactions with people of all sorts. However, in submitting to the vision that God creates for our lives, we will always win in the long run. There is such comfort in knowing that while we are different, we can all be the same in Christ.

Having It Your Way

Our American culture has socialized us to operate in a self-serving spirit. We live in a nation where our self is numero uno (number one). Every day, most people walk right past each other without any concern for the next person. We travel on the train, bus, aircraft, etc., together and many times leave these modes of transportation without ever speaking to our neighbor. We take it a step further by selfishly planning our lives to benefit ourselves only. We make our own plan for building our own empires. However, God says, "Give me your life so that I can bring you into your purpose." As pastor Rick Warren said in his book Purpose Drive Life, "You are not here by accident." We must get it into our heads that God has a plan for our lives. God is holding out his hand saying, "Come if you are tired, broken, confused, or angry." He wants to heal us. He wants to heal you and set you on a path to fulfill your purpose and destiny. If you have it your way, frustration will be your own companion. It is impossible for you to predetermine the consequences of your action. You may be thoroughly trained in forecasting. You may have acquired managerial and leadership skills, but without God, everything will be done without purpose. God's way is the most perfect way. What a joy to simply know that we can rest in peace at night when we go to bed because God is in control. Relinquish your hold on your life, and give God the permission to plan it, order it, and release you to the world. You and I were born to impact the world. You were born to create, build, and to serve. As a leader, I initiate, coordinate, and implement ideas every day in order to make the institutions more effective. Yet every decision is made with consultation, guidance, and direction from God. My steps are ordered by God. Allow God to order your steps.

> Order My Steps in Thy Word and let not any iniquity have dominion over me.
>
> Psalm 119:133 (NKJV)

Power Points of This Chapter

- Doors can only be opened if we are prepared mentally to walk through them.
- Wanting exciting things to happen but unwilling to take the plunge will not serve to move you into maturity.
- Life changes, and we must rise to the occasion and change ourselves.
- Truth, integrity, determination, tenacity, and doing the right thing will enable and empower you to win in the long run.
- Relinquish your hold on your life, and give God the permission to plan it, order it, and release you to the world.

God Will Watch Your Back

> And the angel of God, the one who went before the camp of Israel, moved. And He went to the rear of them. And the pillar of cloud went from in front of their face and it stood behind them.
>
> Exodus 14:19 (NKJV)

Have you ever been undermined by someone you placed your complete confidence in and was later disappointed to learn that your confidence was betrayed? This is painful and can result in bitterness through unforgiveness. A host of other negative consequences may also be the result of betrayal. Betrayal is a major factor that can cause business deals to fall through, friendships to be lost, trust to be broken, marriages to become fragmented, churches to split, employees to be fired, and the list goes on. As a leader, I always make every effort to recruit assistants who will speak on my behalf and represent me well during my absence. Despite my efforts to avoid the nauseating pain of betrayal, I have still fell victim to it. The pain is more intense when it is inflicted by people who we expect to carry and run with our vision. We expect compliments from the ones we love. Yet at times, instead of congratulations, we are subjects of criticism. We are dismayed when we are unable to find our closest companions, friends, supporters, and family members to celebrate with us during our victories.

Many people are driven by their own personal agenda. Every day, people in the business world selfishly work for self-preservation and self-gratification with no intention of empowering their colleagues and counterparts. A selfish lifestyle brings selfish results. I believe that God hates selfishness with a passion. The Egyptians pursued the Israelites for selfish reasons only. They wanted to continue their system of slavery. The Egyptians' grave mistake is that they chose the wrong victim. They decided to pursue the people who were on the path to the promise land. Similarly, Satan's mistake is that he chose to pursue us, God's property. God is obligated to protect his own. The Lord will go to any length to stop the devices of the enemy. We can take solace in the same promise God gave to the Israelites (Hebrews). The Egyptian you see today, you will not see them tomorrow because God is watching every move you make. He walks before you to lead you and stands behind you to protect you. Be consoled and encouraged as the journey continues.

God Will Make a Way of Escape

There are moments in which we may wonder why or even question God regarding the reasons for what may be perceived as unnecessary afflictions. The key factor for such affliction is the simple fact that we, like the Israelites, have made an exodus from Egypt and are advancing to our promised land. Anyone who dares to break out of the box, refuse to conform to the status quo, or question man-made systems will come under the fire of retaliation. There is never a change without a price. Jesus Christ died for all humankind. He paid the ransomed price for our sins with his own blood. He was literally bruised and afflicted. If we desire to be a stalwart of transformation, we must expect pain. The enemy will come after us in hot pursuit because we are valuable to God, to our family, and to society. At times, we forget how precious we are and the invaluable potential we carry around every day to change the world. World changers are average people who God elevates to make a global difference. As we move from a position of mediocrity to a place of excellence, we will notice that Satan is not happy. Do you ever wonder why all hell seems to be breaking loose in your life after you made a decision to change the world? The price we sometimes pay is rejection, ridicule, character assassination, and much more. People who move away from traditional thinking and norms always face scrutiny. I observed the life of a young lady who was an orphan. She grew up in poverty and experienced incest, abuse, and the worst types of conditions that are conceivable. However, during her teenage years, she gave her life to Christ and submitted to the transformational power of the Holy Spirit. There was evidently a mighty call from God on her life. She committed to a personal program of spiritual growth that would transform her life from one of merely getting by to one of excellence. Her challenges were no longer those that came as a result of the pain of her past, but rather, they were challenges that came from those people who she expected to understand her drive and passion. She shared testimonies of the opposition that sometimes came from those who were subordinates, as well as superiors. Even her very role as a female leader was questioned and debated as to whether women should serve in certain capacities. She fought back rejection and ridicule with the love of God. She remained focused and trusted God completely to move her from one place to another. Today, she is a world-renowned evangelist, pastor, author, and spiritual leader. Somewhere in this short story, we can all identify with portions of her journey. It is always God who opens those doors and creates opportunities that deliver us from adverse situations.

Watch Those Words

There is life and death in the power of the tongue. Words cannot be erased, and when they are released, there is always a consequence. Words carry a creative force and power. That's why personal prophetic words spoken of a nation, family, child, or individual must be prayed for and watched. The creative force generated by the spoken word along with faith will bring about change.

Similarly, negative words must be cancelled and rebuked in order to prevent them from coming to pass. Negative words spoken against our lives are probably one of the greatest weapons used in Satan's arsenal. Many children grow into adults and are bound by negative words spoken of their lives by their parents, relatives, colleagues, and others. Imagine the endless verbal insults spoken against the Israelites during slavery. The Egyptians were embarrassed because their words were failing. They quickly realized their mistake, changed their minds, and began to pursue the Israelites. Unbeknownst to the Egyptians, God always makes a way of escape for his people. The spoken word of God, as seen, transformed the impossible into the possible. When the mighty waters of the Red Sea separated, a way of escape was made because of the spoken word. The Hebrews way of escape was also their door to opportunities. The door of opportunity was also the beginning of an awesome relationship with God. We have experiences in our lives, which are similar to that of the Israelites. We must be confident that we will not lose our mind after we decided to move into a life of liberation. I believe that every individual, particularly leaders, must learn to submit, respect, and surrender to the authority of the Word of God. However, there are times when a system becomes outdated and for a multitude of reasons, no longer works and must change. The Word of God, again, encourages change, helps us to embrace change, and will work to change our situations. Satan loves complacency, flourishes in traditional systems, and fights change. The fear of failure causes many people to hold on to what they see rather than exploring uncharted territories. What if Thomas Edison gave up on his inventions? What if he didn't attempt several thousand times to make his discoveries a beneficial reality? How different would our world be? In my personal life, upon reflection, I wonder, "What if I did not follow the voice of God and change my position from a Sunday school teacher to a pastor when called by God?" I stepped out despite my fears. Conquering fear is simply acting despite fear. God has provided many ways of escape for me. It was the Word of God that functioned as the catalyst that initiated my destiny and the glue that preserved order in my life.

Coverage Is Provided: the Cloud and the Fire

I believe supernatural and natural weapons are employed by God to fight the forces of darkness around us. God himself was protecting the children of Israel, but all they could see was cloud at daytime, and pillar of fire by night. Several revelations are evident here. A cloud is a nonthreatening object that blocks the rays of the sun. It provides rain and moves with the wind. This cloud had the ability to transform itself at night to provide light. Interestingly, while the cloud guided the Israelites, it also shielded them from the attack of the enemy. In one instance, the cloud changed its position and stood between Israel and its enemy. God still utilizes natural facets of life to speak to us in many ways. God has the ability to manipulate the forces of nature to fight for us.

I recall one night while driving home from a preaching engagement in New Jersey to my home in New York, I blew a tire out. It was a bad snowstorm that night, and I was stranded on the highway. I slowly maneuvered the car onto the closest exit road and called for help. The most prestigious towing service was contacted. I thought I was rescued, but they said they could only tow my car to a point of safety, which was the nearest public parking lot. I was fifty miles from home, and no help was in sight. Stranded at twelve midnight in a storm without a solution, I would not desire this scenario for anyone. Suddenly, a truck drove up and stopped beside me. A gentleman stepped out of the truck and approached my window. He said that he came to help me. He pulled out a tire from his vehicle. Amazingly, it was the exact size for my car. He successfully changed the tire, and I marveled as he refused to accept payment and was reluctant to provide his identity. That night forever changed my thinking. I knew God sent help during this emergency and not only that, he proved to me that he still works anytime and in any weather. If you dwell where he places you, he will protect you.

> He who dwells in the secret place of the Most High shall rest under the shadow of the Almighty. I will say of Jehovah, my refuge and my fortress; my God in Him I will trust. Surely He will deliver you from the fowler's trap and from the destroying plague. He shall cover you with His feathers, and under His wings you shall trust. His truth shall be your shield and buckler.
>
> Psalm 91:1

We are guaranteed protection by God. Notice in later years when Israel became established politically as a nation, it was their disobedience to God that caused them to be carried into captivity. It was their reluctance to maintain the conditional covenants that served to erode their infrastructure and authority as a leading nation. Any person who maintains a lifestyle of obedience to God's word will last. The humble will be exalted, but the proud will be put down.

You Are a Winner

God looks on the heart and reads our intentions and thoughts every moment. Our colleagues and the world read our inside based on what we project on the outside. It is almost impossible to truly know someone unless you live with that person. Consequently, we are assessed every day by the people we work with, worship with, and associate ourselves with. I am a single African American woman, and as a woman, I don't necessarily fit the description of a pastor and/or a library director. People are stereotyped, misrepresented, and misunderstood every day because of a variety of reasons. It is crucial that we pay close attention to our actions, dress code, and speech because these are three major areas in which others assess us. An attorney dressed like a contractor will send the wrong message. A library director dressed like a garbage collector will send the wrong message. Sometimes, even a pastor dressed completely different from the congregation he or she leads can relay the wrong message. Being cognizant of our environment and how we influence the people we interact with daily will have one of two impacts. Either we will grow and mature with the people around us, or we will diminish and decrease in our influence and our ability to change the world positively. Our attitude can be the catalyst for positive change or negative change in our lives, as well as for the people we lead. As already seen, speaking positive words of comfort and encouragement and decreeing and declaring positive words over our lives can create transformation. The way we see ourselves is directly related to the words we speak. The very moment I was typing this paragraph, one of my daughters walked into my room and declared, "I think I am cursed because nothing is working out for me." My immediate response was to give her this paragraph to read. I explained, "You are what you think you are. Never define your life by your current circumstances. Your future always looks far better than today because you can never lose with God as the director of your life." The psalmist states, "Order my steps Oh Lord and let sin have no dominion over me." Psalm 119:133 (KJV). It is imperative that we maintain a positive outlook on life, even when it appears that we are on the losing side. It is impossible for us to lose when our destinies are already written by the hands of God himself. You and I are winners. We must believe it, know it, act it, say it, and live it. Winners are blessed and not cursed. Winners utilize negative situations for their learning. Winners raise themselves up and bounce back. Winners create stories taken from their diverse negative experiences to help others. Winners never stop moving but keep focused on their destinations.

Power Points of This Chapter

- The creative force generated by the spoken work along with faith will bring about change.

- Negative words spoken against our lives are probably one of the greatest weapons used in Satan's arsenal.
- God looks on the heart and reads our intentions and thoughts every moment.
- World changers are average people who God elevates to make a global difference.

Celebrate Your Victories

> Then the sons of Moses and Israel sang this song to Jehovah, and spoke saying, I will sing to Jehovah, for he has triumphed gloriously, the horse and the rider he has thrown into the sea.
>
> Exodus 15:1 (NKJV)

Cultures, nations, and people everywhere celebrate milestones of achievement. All types of holidays are celebrated worldwide because it is a good thing to keep memories alive. The Israelites are no exception; they took time out to remember the achievements, victories, and good memories of their people. When the Israelites crossed over the Red Sea, it meant that they were liberated, and not only that, but their God had defeated their slave masters with a mighty show of his hands. They were delighted, elated, joyful, and excited that after 430 years, they were free. The impossible was now possible. They were liberated, free at last, out of bondage, free to dream, free to make their own decisions, etc. Moses, Miriam, Joshua, and the thousands who came out now had time to reflect on the events of the past few days. "Did it really happen?" they must have asked. "Are we really over the Red Sea?" It must have taken a little while to digest the fact that what their fore-parents were unable to accomplish, even though they prayed for it, had materialized. Recently,

I baptized a sixty-year-old woman. She was sick, spent some time in the hospital, and shared her testimony of how she was delivered. She was diagnosed with a very serious skin disease. One Sunday morning, she woke up and remembered that I had started a church in Ossining, New York, some seven years ago. She heard a voice directing her to wake up, take the train, and search for the church. She got dressed, caught the bus from New York City, another train to Ossining, then walked from the train station to a home of a relative she remembered. She was then given directions to the church, found it, and responded to the call of God. She was baptized the following Sunday and testified days later that she could not believe the changes in her life. She spoke of the emotional, psychological, and spiritual changes she experienced. She changed her hairstyle, purchased new clothing, and came back to church with an entire makeover. She found God. She was liberated from years of bondage. She could not describe the dramatic change in her life. It was time to celebrate.

Let's Sing a New Song

Moses and Miriam recognized that it was time to celebrate. The Israelites brought out the tambourines, the trumpets, and other kinds of instruments and began to praise God. Our praises are probably the most powerful weapons against the enemy. If we wake up every day with an attitude of praise, imagine how our lives would be transformed. Praises are happy moments when we say them with a grateful heart. Thank you, God, for your grace and mercy. Every day should be a day of thanksgiving, even when everything is not going exactly the way we desire. Learning to praise God at all times invokes God's presence and causes God to dwell in our midst. Try waking up every morning with a smile on your face, praise in your mouth, and a dance in your feet. You will witness how these seemingly simple actions will transform your life. Your frown will be changed to a smile; your problems will appear so much smaller because God's presence is invited. Praises will fill your heart with the peace of God. How reassuring it is to know that God is with us every moment, particularly in the times of trouble.

I have personally received deliverance over and over during times of trouble because of my attitude toward God on recollection, it was during these very same times of trouble that I received a promotion on my job from a department head to the director of the facility. I received a salary increase of twenty thousand dollars and was called out by God to preach the gospel. My greatest victories came when I praised. I believe that the windows of heaven open and respond to a grateful heart. It is not time to cry but to laugh. Medically, laughing and smiling, despite our horrors in life, ushers in healing to the body and mind. Even during times of crisis, I have learned to laugh. Laugh your way through your troubles because the joy of the Lord is your strength. Stop complaining and whining about your troubles, but rather, take some time periodically to show gratitude by saying thanks to God with your praises. Lift your hands and thank God, and you will see results. Laugh your way through it! Right now, if you can, stand. Lift your hands toward the ceiling or the sky and repeat these words: "Thank you, Lord, for all your benefits unto me. Thank you for waking me this morning. Thank you for life. Thank you for the victory. Thank you for my family, friends, and for everything you have permitted me to go through. I do not understand everything, but the joy of the Lord is my strength." Now, hold your head and your hands up, and dance if you can. Do you notice the immediate transformation? You feel better because you have just released your negative energy to God, and he in turn has just entered into your space and has filled it with his love, mercy, and joy. Presently, I am faced with major challenges in the ministry. However, I have taken the time to encourage someone else as I take a walk, sit in my garden, and read the word of God. I'm focusing on the promises that God has made to me. I may have to wait, but sooner or later, I will see the results.

You Are No Longer a Slave

One of the greatest benefits of emancipation from slavery is the ability to own property. Slaves die without the ability to leave an inheritance because they have never become owners of property. In every free society throughout history, owning land is one of the basic rights of a citizen. All rights are removed from a person when they become the property of a slave master. The desire to own another person is a wicked conception. Satan is the greatest slave master throughout history. He has managed to fool millions into believing that his benefits offered are permanent. The truth behind his deception is that what he has presented them with is a short term loan. On the other side of the pendulum, God's benefits are forever. God provides us with genuine freedom in him. God's freedom not only provides us with an opportunity to own property, but also to have the legal right to leave an inheritance. God has given everyone the opportunity to receive a permanent inheritance not only here on this earth but also in heaven. We are entitled because we are sons and daughters of God. Jesus promised that he is going to prepare us a place, that where he is, there we may be also. We must know who we are and understand that we are free to think, to dance, to laugh, and to exercise our rights as citizens of heaven and earth.

> But seek first the kingdom of God and his righteousness and all these things shall be added unto you.
>
> Matthew 6:33 (NKJV)

Jesus declared if we voluntarily and willingly allow him to be our king and live under his domain, he will bless us right here on this planet. In addition to all the things that the world seeks, God will endow us with eternal life. What a consolation to know that our father is the King of kings, owns everything, and has provided for us an abundant inheritance.

Maintain a Lifestyle of Joy

Most of us do not set aside sufficient time to celebrate. Celebration sends a mighty signal to your enemies and friends alike that there is victory. I recently told someone that it appears that I do not have adequate time in my busy life to celebrate the small victories. Some great things have happened to me lately, which I know are direct results of my obedience to God and my faithful service to his kingdom. However, I find that I have the tendency to give thanks without stopping to have planned celebrations. We must be strategic about our times of celebration. We must set aside some time in our schedules and calendars to do nothing but celebrate our victories. Life is short, very short, when you get to age fifty. Grandchildren are born to some of us. Children get married and graduate from college. They grow up and join the work force. The face of our church, family, and jobs in the secular change; and before long, everything seems to be moving too rapidly. We oftentimes get caught up in the moment and in the flow of things, and suddenly, if we are not careful, we wake up one day and life slips right by us and is gone. It is critical that we realize that what matters most are the memories we create from those great moments we spend with our friends and family. Stress is an issue for most of us who practice and maintain a busy lifestyle and is compounded by the fact that we do not create opportunities to replenish. As we will see later, we can replenish by laughing, spending private time in the presence of God, or simply just do nothing. We must plan for relaxation intentionally with the same fervency as we plan our work goals and objectives and make time to execute them. We are overwhelmed because we do not have enough fun time, sleep time, and downtime. Every hardworking pastor needs a Sabbath. One of the greatest Sabbath days for church leaders are Mondays, a day when the entire world is hard at work and buzzing with activities, but the man and woman of God is in respite. Our world has become way too busy. We have overbooked our schedules and have complicated our lives in a million different ways. Consequently, we operate on empty and do not have adequate reserves of spiritual, emotional, and psychological energy to deal with the negatives generated from the very lives that we lead. Many of us suffer from an array of medical issues brought about by burnout. We constantly give our reserves of energy but receive very little in return. I am quickly learning to step back, remove myself, and be deliberate in maintaining my joy. The Hebrews celebrated but did not strategically maintain their joy. The moment they had the next major challenge, they were ready to stone Moses, their leader. Why? They did not develop a joyful lifestyle.

Maintain the Right Attitude: Manage Your Emotions

Our emotional health is critical to our development and indeed to our successful arrival to our place of promise. Our emotions have direct bearing on our attitudes. Again, the Hebrews failed in their ability to maintain composure and diplomacy during times of crisis. They became expert complainers and whiners and had very little sympathy or respect for the great leader given to them by God. We must spend some time to explore this concept because it was the emotional state of the people that resulted in their demise. A whole new generation of people inherited the promised land. Those who left Egypt died along the way with the exception of Joshua and Caleb. The attitudes of these two men differentiated them from the rest of the crowd. They were positive thinkers, extremely confident, even during times of crisis, and submitted to Moses in humility and obedience. They had teachable spirits and stood out from among the majority. How could the attitude of an entire nation rob them of their destiny, one may ask? During times when they should respectfully seek God for solutions, they responded by grumbling. During learning opportunities, they ran away from the presence of God. During difficulties, they distrusted God with their negative responses to the leader that was placed over them.

Emotions can be defined as feelings grounded in the mind, both of excitement, pain or anxiety. It can further be defined as a conscious state of joy, sorrow, fear, anger, love, jealousy, etc. Our actions, as humans, are driven by our emotional state. For instance, if love is one of the emotions and we practice love in all aspects of our lives, we will live to see its effect on those around us. Similarly, if we live in an angry state, we will see the results of a life that is ruled by anger. Although feelings can be very strong and demanding, we do not have to let them rule our lives. We can learn to manage our emotions rather than allowing them to manage us. If we have to wait to see how we feel before we know we can enjoy the day, then we are giving our feelings control over us. But thankfully, we have free will and can make decisions that are not based on our feelings. If we are willing to make right choices regardless of how we feel, God will always be faithful to give us the strength to do so. Understanding our feelings, as well as controlling them, is quite important. Happiness is an emotion that fosters well-being, and I believe it is contagious. We should not deny our emotions. Instead, we only need to learn to control them. It is important that you understand that I am not saying you should deny your emotions, only deny them the right to control you. It seems emotions have a mind of their own. If your health is not good, if you are told by the doctor that you have a disease, your emotions only scream louder. It will be easier if you don't let your emotions run wild. The more you stay in control of your emotions, the better your decisions will be.

The human personality consists of roughly four-fifths emotions and one-fifth intellect. This means that our decisions are made on the basis of 80 percent emotions and 20 percent intellect or reason. Those of us who are driven by our emotions consequently make the wrong choices in life. We must note the following:

- Proactive choices made without too much emotional involvement will help us regain control of our lives.
- Controlling our thought life will help us to control our emotions. The average person has 70,000 thoughts every day, and many of those thoughts trigger a corresponding emotion.
- Talk about our positive experiences rather than the negative in order to support and amplify our positive emotions.

- Talk about the positive feelings so that they will increase and negative feelings will lose their strength.

Feelings in and of themselves are neither good nor bad. They are just unstable and must be managed. For instance, a child wants the right to do anything but does not understand the danger involved. It becomes the responsibility of the parents to control that child. Likewise, we must parent our emotions; we must train them to serve us so that we don't become their slaves. Out-of-control emotions wear you out and leave you angry, guilty, frustrated, and confused. As a result, you lose your problem solving ability, become overwhelmed, and eventually burn out from insufficient rest.

Guard Your Heart

The heart is the seat of the emotions. Once God has control of the heart and we operate with the heart of God, we consequently have power over our emotions. God's heart is humble. God's heart is peaceful. God's heart is kind. God's heart is honest. Every action begins in the heart. This is the area where decisions are made. The heart has to be guarded by God and the Holy Spirit. It is the wellspring of our being. Let us guard negative thoughts and emotions from entering our hearts. Along the journey, we learn to grow and mature to develop the character and nature of God. Let's not accept what the devil is saying about us. He says that your negative emotions are a part of our personality and that's the way we should be. For example: "I have to speak my mind. I can't let anyone walk over me. I have rights, and I am an adult. I have feelings, and I have to be able to express myself. I have to speak the truth and stand up for myself." Instead of following what the devil says, we must say, "I am on a journey with God. I have to be like him. I have to feel like him. I have to act like him. I must portray his attributes, his characteristics. I must ask God to create a new heart in me, as well as renew a right spirit in me." We cannot be trapped in our habits, our culture, and our environment. It has to be God's way, or we will be destroyed along the way. Let's wake up and say, "Enough is enough." Let's allow God to transform us by giving him a chance. When God transforms us, he does it well. We will be a vessel ready to be used by him. Spiritual maturity cannot be accomplished until and unless we surrender our emotions completely in total obedience. Then his purpose and design for our lives will be fulfilled. In the book entitled Change Agent, Os Hillman states that, "to be a godly change agent, you must live from the heart, not performance. God wants to relate to each of us through a heart connection, not through our performance. Our motivation to obey should be rooted in our heart connection to our heavenly father."

Power Points of This Chapter

- The windows of heaven open and respond to a grateful heart.

- Every day should be a day of thanksgiving, even when everything is not going exactly the way we desire.
- Laugh your way through your troubles because the joy of the Lord is your strength.

PART 2

THE WILDERNESS

In the Wilderness with a Promise

> And the whole congregation of the sons of Israel murmured against Moses and Aaron in the wilderness. And the sons of Israel said to them, Oh that we had died by the hand of Jehovah in the land of Egypt when we sat by the flesh-pots, when we ate bread to the full! For you have brought us forth into this wilderness to kill this whole assembly with hunger.
>
> Exodus 16:2–3 (NKJV)

The Red Sea was behind the children of Israel. They celebrated their crossing over and gave God thanks for the victory. Shortly after, however, their mood shifted away from celebration. They had entered the wilderness. The wilderness is defined as a desert or a tract of land or region that's uncultivated and uninhabitable by a human. They were now positioned in a place with minimal resources. There was no food and certainly none sufficient to feed over a million people. The little provisions they took along with them, by this time, had been exhausted. They were now in it for the long haul. They were either going to survive by the help of God or die in the wilderness from hunger. In addition to being faced with starvation, they were surrounded by wild animals. The wilderness is home to some of most vicious predators. They faced snakes, sand dunes, and treacherous paths, which lay ahead of them.

It was now time for another test. They were deliberately placed in the wilderness for a reason. The wilderness was their place of testing and training. Their leader, Moses, had some training when he spent forty years as a shepherd working for his father-in-law, Jethro. However, no one else was equipped with desert training. They had no clue how to survive in the wild. Nevertheless, they were placed in this awful place in order to advance into the promise. They were in the wilderness with a promise. A promise from God represents his words spoken over our lives. God does not think as we do in terms of time and space. We sometimes forget that when the right time comes, God will bring his promise to pass. Most often our timing is off. God shows up when we are not prepared or ready. When we least expect it, God works on our behalf. Looking at the journey of the children of Israel from start to finish, we will notice that God supplied their needs partly by ordinary and occasionally by miraculous means. They ate manna for forty years, and the manna stopped only at the point of entry into the promised land. They never lacked clothing, shelter, and food. The wilderness is not a time of plenty; it is a time when God chooses to satisfy our basic needs while we are being taught great lessons. Let us examine some of the stops that God created for them shortly before and during the wilderness experience:

Succoth:	A place of booth
Etham:	A place of strength
Pihahiroth:	To be shut in
Morah:	Bitter wells/affliction

Elim:	A park or paradise with springs and palms
Wilderness of Sin:	Manna was given here
Alush:	Lion's den
Rephidim:	A place of refreshing
Sinai:	Glowing heat
Kibroth:	Graves of lust, craving, and gluttony
Hazeroth:	Fenced enclosures where Miriam was punished

Can you see that the long list of places God introduced to them each represented a new experience? Trouble was inevitable because one of the tools God utilizes to test his people is the tool of adversity. During times of adversity, God gives us just enough to survive the rough times. He observes us closely to see our reaction to the positions we are placed in. It is said that experience teaches wisdom. As God is colorful and believes in a variety, so he, in turn, introduces us to a variety of situations and circumstances. Morah, for instance, the place of bitter wells, represents affliction. I have not yet seen a mature person who has not testified about their place of affliction. Morah are the times when we feel pain of one sort or another because of sickness, broken relationships, death, divorce, and all sorts of crisis. However, Morah is not permanent; it is only a stop on the journey, a necessary one. Morah is a place of trouble where we mature and grow and become more appreciative of that which God has placed in our lives. This place humbles us and converts us from arrogant people to a people with a heart, exercising compassion for others. Remember the life of David, a Hebrew who God called to lead the Israelites. He came from humble beginnings as a shepherd boy but was chosen by God because he had an excellent heart. David was recognized by King Saul as a great leader even though he was not serving in any significant capacity. Satan recognized that great destiny was pronounced upon the life of David when he was anointed by the Prophet Samuel. Saul was serving as king but was fired by God because of disobedience. It is possible for someone to be fired by God but continue to serve in their place. David went through a period of great testing when he was literally chased by King Saul on recognition that the future king would not be someone from Saul's direct line but rather David. This was a time of character building for David. He did not curse God but used this time of bitterness to cry out to God for help. He drew closer to God during this period more than any other time in his life and was ready for the elevation to king when the time came. His place of trouble contributed significantly to his personal and spiritual development. His skills as a soldier were sharpened. He learned intimacy with God. He developed his leadership skills and acquired the training that was necessary to keep him where he was going to be placed later in his journey.

Wait on the Lord: It's a Process

I do not enjoy visiting the doctor, particularly my gynecologist whose waiting period is about four hours. This doctor is noted to be one of the best surgeons in the northeast of America. He specializes in his field and also delivers babies in the same hospital. Thus, he has emergency cases going on all day. As a result, the wait time is exacerbating. The first time I visited, I was appalled at the waiting period. However, I was delightfully amazed when I received my turn because he was an excellent communicator and did his job extremely well. I was tempted to walk out of the doctor's office, but I would have not been seen by the doctor and would have lost the opportunity to meet a great person. After becoming even more acquainted with him, I realized that the wait was worth it. God too expects us to wait. However, when we wait on the Lord, he renews our strength. Sometimes, you may see your colleagues and friends getting blessed and wonder to yourself, "How did I get left out of the equation again?" You may ask yourself when you are going to see your new car, new home, graduate from school, have some money in the bank, etc. I remember days when I could hardly make ends meet. My three children would go to school without lunch and wait until they returned home to have a meal. I would think to myself, "When are they going to grow up? Will this ever end? God must not like me to allow me to experience these things." Now I can look back with a grateful heart and give God thanks that I did not return to a symbolic Egypt. I now have the house, car, and too much food. My children have grown up and are getting married. I even have grandchildren. The wait was worth it. Someone may ask the question, "How can I wait in the wilderness?" It's the worst place to wait. But do we really have a choice? There are times when we are without options. At those trying times, we are unable to take things into our own hands. If we were to take them into our own hands, frustration would ensue, and the wrong decisions would be made.

Waiting is never easy, but it is necessary and vital to where you are going. Any mature person who is considered successful will verify that those periods when they had to sit and wait until their goals materialized were invaluable. They respect those days and moments not as empty and void moments but as learning periods. I observe many young ambitious preachers in the church who seek for the limelight early in their walk with God. They invest a great deal of time and energy into their personal ministries by giving great speeches, sermons, publishing books, making record deals, and developing television programs, all surrounding themselves. I also observe them as they aim to begin from the top rather than learning lessons of patience, obedience, tolerance, and character building. Many get discouraged because their plans did not come to fruition, while others get discouraged because they fail in their attempts to make it big. God demotes many because their gifts simply were not able to keep them where they were. It is the strength and stamina that we build in those periods of waiting that keep us at the highest points in our lives.

Run with Patience: There Are Many Miles Ahead

I returned, and saw under the sun, that the race is not to the swift, nor the battle to the strong, neither yet bread to the wise, nor yet riches to men of understanding, nor yet favor to men of skill; but time and chance happens to them all.

Ecclesiastes 9:11 (KJV)

Grumbling and complaining signifies an indifference to the wilderness. The Israelites were people who were not afraid to express their feeling of indifference. They developed a habit of complaining and comparing their current experience with where they came from. In addition, they did not cooperate whenever things were not going their way. They compared the food of Egypt pretty quickly to that of the wilderness. They expressed disregard for Moses who was doing everything possible to put them at ease. Rather than cooperating, they rebelled. Saint Paul, in his writings, admonished his readers not to use them as an example. We can lengthen the wilderness journey by expressing the wrong attitude. On the flip side of the coin, we can go through it without complaining with our promise land on the horizon. In my lifetime, I have seen more self-proclaiming Christians grumbling and complaining than non-Christians. Many dedicated church members are unable to shift their Sunday approach to God to their reality of Monday. My attitude is that if God allows something, then there must be a lesson in it. Associating with people who spend their time attacking leaders will only serve to destroy people with potential. If you desire to be excellent, respect leaders and anyone else who is in charge. There is a reason why God chose Moses and not Aaron to be the commander in chief. That should be respected. Think of the turtle as it glides across the sands of the seashore. It travels over each grain, rock, and debris, and observes it all. Eventually, the turtle arrives at its destination, accomplishing its purpose. Do not shortchange yourself. Be patient, take a deep breath, build your stamina, and run slowly. Life is like a marathon race. Many great runners will drop out on the way from exhaustion. However, you can make it if you endure.

Getting to Know God in a Better Way

The journey is a process. God's desire is for everyone to gain experience along the way. The process is designed to bring us into a closer relationship with God. Each stop must be a lesson, and each lesson draws us closer to God. God can only get closer to us when we invite him. We were created with a free will. We are not God's puppets but people who were designed with the ability to make choices. We decide whether to invite God into our circumstances or walk away from him. During my own experiences, I have learned that a personal invitation must be extended to him. I not only asked for help, I requested consultation. It's like having an attorney, who is the expert on all legal matters, yet you refuse to call him for help, despite being faced with the greatest legal crisis in your life.

God has the blueprint for every challenge we face in life. The Bible is the secret and the authority on all matters. The Bible provides direction for planning to start a new business, returning to complete college, starting a family, planning for the future, etc. The Bible is the answer to humankind's dilemmas. I have proven over and over again that getting to know God in a better way opens a stored basket of wisdom, which can be applied to everyday decision making. The power of prayer has been proven by millions across the planet. Prayer brings us in close communication with God. It is a time when we are able to speak to God, and God responds. I love to wait in prayer to hear God's voice as he gives direction and answers. We can choose to become bitter from pain and resentment, or we can choose life. It is said that great ministries are birthed out of pain. Yet I say that great ministries are birthed out of pain that is given to God. During our times of trials, it is actually the act of bringing God into the situation that turns it around. His presence heals quickly and replaces pain with his anointing. In fact, pain brings us closer to him. There are times when I am unable to pray audibly because of the intense grief. Thus, I groan, cry, or remain silent in his presence. Nevertheless, God understands nonverbal communication just as well. The spirit of God residing in us also makes groaning and utterances we do not understand but God does. Remember, the journey is designed only to bring us closer to God. The stops along the way were not meant to destroy us but to perfect us. What a joy it is to know that our steps are ordered by God. God walks with me every day, even during the moments when I feel alone and isolated. Someone said to me recently, "I don't feel as if God is hearing me when I pray." My response was: "You don't need to feel God's presence physically at all times. The Lord is simply stretching your faith like a rubber band. When it's necessary, God will overwhelm you with his presence. All you need to do is just continue to stay focused. Keep praying, keep believing, keep trusting, and keep moving towards your goal."

Living On Manna: Angel's Food

> Consider the lilies see how they grow, they toil not, yet Solomon in all His glory was not arrayed like one of these
>
> Luke 12:27 (KJV)

Do you realize that God provided manna for the entire journey of the children of Israel? From start to finish, they were given just enough to sustain them. On entering the promised land, the manna stopped immediately. It was not coincidental that they were told to gather just enough for the day and on the Sabbath enough for two days. There is an important principle here that was being implemented. In Matthew chapter five, Jesus spoke to the people concerning food, clothes, and shelter. It was the same principle Jesus spent some time explaining. Many of us become stressed over the basic amenities of life when God has already made provision for all of us who are a part of his kingdom. Manna was a special food created by God for his people. I believe that it may not have looked like much, but all the basic ingredients were included. This special provision was food directly sent from heaven for a people specially chosen. Do you sometimes experience special provision when God gives you just enough to pay the rent or mortgage, just enough to cover your needs? This may be because you are now in a season of wilderness where you are not given an outpouring but just enough. The test of faith is to believe God for tomorrow because he gives you just enough for today. You may not see where the funds or resources for tomorrow will come from, but you know deep down that it will work out somehow. This is a special time, so do not be jealous of your friends, colleagues, neighbors, or coworkers who appear to be living in a place of plenty. Be content in whatever position you find yourself in because our God knows all and is our source. During your period of just enough, you will grow and flourish in a multiplicity of ways. Lately, I have been giving sacrificially to the building project in my church. As the senior pastor, I believe that I must lead by example. So I gave most of my retirement savings, all the funds from my short-term savings, and all the money I set aside from my personal investments. As a result, for some time, I was unable to purchase some of the things I would like. Many times I could not find enough to cover all my bills. One time, I was a little upset about it because it appeared that God did not ask others to give everything. Then I remembered that I asked God to give me a double portion of his blessings. I may not see the blessings as yet, but I know that they're on the way. My faith in God has doubled, and my faith will bring about the double portion in the long run. Thank God for the wisdom to make the sacrifice. Manna is angel's food; it will provide supernatural blessings and sustenance for the journey.

Going around in Circles

The children of Israel went around in circles in the wilderness when God intended for them to go through it. For forty years, they went around in circles repeating the same experiences over and over yet never learning the lessons. As mentioned previously, only Joshua and Caleb entered the promised land. Everyone else died along the way. Why did all of this happen? This was unnecessary and a waste of God's provision. First, we must understand that we cannot bully our way into our promise. Neither can we manipulate the intentions of God. Some people have the mentality of a microwave. Everything must happen quick and fast with the least amount of energy expended.

One of the most powerful forces that can propel us into our destiny is obedience. Obedience is following the requests, commands, or desires of God. Our relationship with God is similar to that of the parent and child. The child has its own opinion, desires, and aspirations, but it doesn't matter because the parent is the leader who has the authority to make the decisions in the home. The child's responsibility is to follow the directives of the parent. The parent provides protection, peace of mind, food, clothing, etc. A child in rebellion will probably get thrown out of the house and may never inherit the possessions of the parent. Our attitude toward God can either make us or break us. How can a parent bless a child who is disrespectful, unwilling to obey the rules of the home? The answer is obvious. A Jamaican anecdote says, "The humblest calf sucks the most milk." The child that is most obedient will reap the greatest rewards from the parent. Building a foundation of respect and accountability in our personal lives will help us to weather any storm. If we choose to respect God and leadership, even when we do not understand what is going on, we will eliminate unnecessary pain. Oh, what needless pain we sometimes bear all because we do not carry everything to God in prayer. A circle represents an endless cycle of events consisting of the same things happening over and over. If things appear to be this way for you, then you must identify the reasons for the cycle. There may probably be something that is not being done to stop the cycle. Perhaps God is directing you to worship him instead of focusing on the wrong people or aspects of life, which can become idolatry. It could be that someone else or something else is taking the place of God in your life. God is jealous and wants to be first in everything we do. Do not waste time in disobedience. The result will only be a cycle that may lead to spiritual death. You must not forget you are in the wilderness with a promise.

Power Points of This Chapter

- When you least expect God to work on your behalf, he shows up to change the situation.
- The test of faith is to believe God for tomorrow because he gives you just enough for today.
- If we choose to respect God and leadership, even when we do not understand what is going on, we will eliminate unnecessary pain.

- Building a foundation of respect and accountability in our personal lives will help us to weather any storm.

Rephidim: A Place of Refreshing

> Behold I will stand before you there on the Rock in Horeb, and you shall strike the rock, and water will come out of it, that the people may drink.
>
> Ex. 17:7 (KJV)

If you are feeling tired, broken, overwhelmed, and dissatisfied with the experiences of life as you read this book, I would like to inform you that there is good news. Life comes with curve balls, and as I was told by my mentor, everyone experiences crisis at some point in their life. For some of us, it may be early, while for others, it may be later in their life. The bottom line is life under the sun comes with heartbreaks and laughter. We have our sad moments and happy moments. We must remain focused and take things in stride because God is always in control.

There is relief for anyone and everyone who believe that God's grace is sufficient to keep them particularly when there is no solution or answer in sight. It is very possible to recover from a state of tiredness, weariness, depression, and exhaustion simply by taking time to replenish. Every human being has the capacity to do so much and no more. Our lifestyles in America is one of constant rush. People everywhere are busy juggling family, jobs, church responsibilities, extracurricular activities, and an array of duties, responsibilities, and tasks that leave us in exhaustion at the end of every day. We sometimes attend workshops, seminars, and sessions on how to manage time and discipline ourselves to stick to our schedule. Most of the time, we admit none of these things work for the majority of us. I propose that there is a better way and a more workable way to be healed from the many anomalies we are confronted with on the journey. Recently, a colleague on my job shared the story of her four-year-old granddaughter with pride. She is enjoying life as a grandparent and sometimes share the family jokes in the office to lighten our day. On this occasion, she mentioned that her lovely granddaughter said, "Today, I have to attend rehearsal for my class recital, then I have to compete for my school in the cheerleading class, then I have to get my hair done, and the list goes on." Needless to say, the four-year-old was being trained early to be busy just as her parents are busy.

Most people don't know how to stop, relax, and replenish. Like the car that needs gasoline, so we are made by God to refill on spiritual things, as well as natural things. We must remember that we need more than food to survive and to enjoy our lives. We need prayer, sleep, and time-out when we do nothing. Our lives have become complicated, chaotic, and disconnected from God and the people who matter. We must return to simplicity by discarding the junk we have accumulated and proactively seek to maintain the right perspective. God gives the right perspective to anyone who is brave enough to take the risk with him. He leads us with his own hands from one point to another and indeed from one place to another. Let's release the reigns to him and let him take the wheel and steer us in any direction he chooses. Every experience I have gathered along the way, whether they were negative or positive, has served to bring me to a point of maturity. God visited me in the lowest point in my life and reminded me that he cared and that he was going to use me in a mighty way in the future. At the moment I felt abandoned and useless, an array of emotions coursed through my confused mind. But somewhere deep down in my soul, I knew that I was going to get out and that my future would be bright.

I am no exception to the rule. God has a plan for every human being that he has created. He has a promised land, a place right here, right now, where we can experience his peace. From a material point of view, you may not have all the things you desire, but you can have peace now. That's the secret. The only secret to success is in God. Every human being needs a Sabbath. The best example of a Sabbath is to take one day out of every week to relax and to do things that will promote healing only. Everyone, from time to time, must invest extra time in a special project or activity; however, after completion, it is essential that we return to a disciplined approach to downtime. I am not, of course, speaking about a Sabbath that is a religious day, which is set aside for worship. I am talking about a scheduled time that is taken to be alone with God. It is paramount that we invest in our healing by taking time to rest in the presence of God. This special stop, Rephidim, was a place where God wanted to remove the exhaustion and the tiredness created by the previous experiences. This is the place where the people contended with Moses. There was no water for them to drink, and they demanded that Moses give them water to drink. They did not ask pleasantly, but as described by Moses, they almost stoned him for their situation. Oh, how easy it is to blame others for our misfortunes, particularly the person in charge. On the other hand, it is critical that we take responsibility for our actions and understand that our destiny is in the hands of God and not on our leader in the church or on the job. It is indeed God who provides and prospers.

They again reflected on Egypt and blamed Moses for their unpleasant situation. The journey of life will make us exhausted periodically, especially when we are dealing with a series of crisis all at the same time. In the year, 2012, I lost several relatives all during the same time. Within a matter of a few months, there were four deaths in my family. My brother, one of my favorite relatives, passed away in Jamaica. I took time off from my fulltime position and travelled to be with the rest of the family for one week. The moment I returned, my brother-in-law passed away in England. When I thought it was over, shortly after, my adopted daughter called me on my way home from my office to announce that her birth mother who resides in the same community was lying in the street with ambulances surrounding her. Needless to say, my daughter lost her mother within minutes. One moment she was with us, and in another moment, she was gone. Death creates stress just like financial problems, loss of jobs, sickness, and the like. Yet, I have proven that we can be refreshed in our private moments with God as we reflect on his word, listen to his voice, and share our pain with him. Rather than sharing how we feel with our colleagues, church members, and the people around us, there is a far better way. Telling someone about our concerns and feelings will aid for a while but will not provide the kind of long-term, lasting healing that we need. We are no use to ourselves and others if we live our lives on the edge; waking up constantly tired and exhausted is a dishonor to our creator and ourselves. The cycle of neglect of ourselves can be broken when we strategically plan to replenish on the things that really matter. What matters most is that we enjoy life and forget the past, including the experiences of yesterday.

Yes. To a certain extent, we are made by history—yesterday. But tomorrow is always brighter as we live with hope that the latter will always be more glorious than the past. It is remarkable how God can successfully take on any project and bring it to completion. The journey from Egypt to the promise land was a project that was designed, monitored, and controlled by God. It was initiated by God and completed by God, and anything he starts, he will absolutely complete.

Notice it was the people's fault why many did not finish the journey. It was their reluctance to learn from their experiences. It was their neglect to develop a personal relationship with the only one who could defeat the giants that led to their demise along the way. The journey was meant to be enjoyed. It was not meant to be an avenue or reason to complain. It was never meant to destroy anyone that was a part of the group chosen. The journey was meant for their education, learning, success, experience, and enjoyment. Those who began blew the greatest opportunity of a lifetime and failed to see from the outset that the promise land was there ready and waiting to receive them. Enjoy the journey.

Arise for the Work Is Great

> Moses my servant is dead, now therefore arise, go over this Jordan, you and all this people, to the land which I am giving to them-the children of Israel.
>
> Joshua 1:2 (KJV)

Against all odds, we can make it. Today, I have very little tolerance for individuals who fail to recognize the benefits of hard work. We must be aware, however, that sometimes hard work does not necessarily pay off in the long run. It is, however, a better choice to work hard than to be lazy. According to Bishop T.D. Jakes, "We must fight strategically for the prize we long to enjoy. We must invest our energy in direct connection to our goals. It's a mistake to believe that hard work always yields great results." I recently spoke to a group of teachers and students at my Bible college's annual convocation. My subject was taken from the book of Haggai chapter two. The focus of my presentation was on the value of hard work and teamwork. In the text, the prophet spoke to three categories of individuals and encouraged them to be strong and work. This was a period in Israel's history when the nation was no longer a nation but was subject to a foreign king and had very little resources to work with to accomplish the giant task of rebuilding the temple. God knew their hearts and saw the discouragement and the fact that they were reflecting on the glory of the previous temple. The prophet was told to refocus them by encouraging them to be strong and work. I took the liberty to apply exegesis and show that God wanted them to be mentally strong, as well as physically strong. The reason for this was to prepare them to work together under duress to accomplish the work at hand. There are several factors working here that must be applied if we are going to make it against all odds. We must be able to remain focused.

As a senior pastor and library director with great responsibilities, it is critical that during times when problematic situations arise, I must remain focused. I must see my destination at all times. I see it but must, at the same time, understand that I cannot live my life based on the fact that I know where I am going. I must work every day despite what's happening around me. We must have a few good people in our lives. A support system is necessary in order to get over hurdles and make the right decisions. Notice in the same scripture the prophet spoke to the governor, the priest, and the people. Three completely different, broad skill sets were needed at this time in order to complete the task at hand. The administrative, business, and political skill sets the spiritual abilities and aptitudes, as well as the variety of skills from the common people. Everyone had to strengthen themselves physically and mentally and work as a great team to accomplish rebuilding the temple. Os Hillman states in his book *Change Agent*, "Each of us was created to solve a problem." No one was born by accident, and therefore, no one should live aimlessly. It is true that some of us must work harder than others to become successful, probably based on our family history, background and culture, ethnic group, etc. However, with great determination and following the journey designed by God, we can get to our destination. My past experiences, however, became the driving force that motivated me to excel. I was only twelve years old when I made the decision that I wanted to be successful. I was determined to do well and to help as many people as possible to do the same. I am determined to leave a legacy; that's my purpose.

I was only eighteen years old when I married. Within five years, I gave birth to my three children. I knew I made a grave mistake after only two months, but I decided I was in it for the long haul. I must share this moment of the journey when I checked myself into college with two babies. I had no car, no stroller, no one to journey with when I took my two babies over fifty miles to their grandparents to babysit while I attended school. This journey was done once or twice per week. In addition, while I studied later at the University of the West Indies, I journeyed every week to visit my three children at their grandparents' home. I graduated with honors under extreme circumstances from both colleges. The story continues; I left my country to seek for greener grass in the United States like everyone else. I ended up in Buffalo without proper winter gear and clothing during the middle of winter, January 20. I resided with my professor who, within months, gave my room and space to my best friend and left me without a proper place to live. I was told that I should take a break from school and accumulate the funds to start later. My answer was adamantly and resoundingly no. I graduated with my master's degree within one year and completed that phase of the journey. I paid for college by cleaning homes, working in nursing homes, and with the help of my loving sister and Aunt Una, who was the foundation of the family. It is impossible for anyone to make it on their own without an infrastructure of people who see your potential.

I recently counseled one of the young ladies I mentored. I encouraged her to invest in her education. "Money spent on education is not money counted," I stated. While we must be fiscally responsible, it is always better to take the risk of investing in a skill or a profession. Ten years of education will guarantee a better future. Failure is neglecting to begin the journey, failure is refusing to take the risk, and failure is remaining at the beginning of the journey and refusing to take the step forward. Keep moving one foot in front of each other because the idea is to get from here to there. Always aim to move from point A to point B. I oftentimes ask myself the question "What next?" I oftentimes ask God the question "Where next?" Every step involves work. Arise means to be stirred up. It means to be motivated. It means to be encouraged and to come alive. God commanded Joshua to arise at the worst moment of his life. He and the people around him were grieving for the greatest leader in their history. They had more than enough reasons to give up, murmur again, and reflect on their glorious past. They were positioned for greatness, right on the brink of their breakthrough, right on the borders of their promise. But they were blinded by their current circumstance. Oh, how easy it is for us to work long and hard for an extended period of time and just when we are on the brink of the greatest revelation, the greatest success, the greatest season in our lives were stopped and refused to move any further. But I declare that now is your time, now is your season. You may be grieving right now, but God is saying arise. He is saying be strong and be very courageous, that you can do it because your latter is greater than your former. The end of the journey is just across the River Jordan. You are right there, and any moment now you will find rest. If you are a leader in any capacity, you have a responsibility to lead effectively. People are expecting you to be motivated. It is the tenacity, determination, and drive that you portray that will in turn serve to provide you with the necessary support you need. Like Moses or Joshua, you take your queue from God; you receive, replenish, and restore and in turn, move the people collectively into their destination. Yes, there will always be those who are challenging in their behavior and attitude, but you speak volume when you remain motivated and keep working.

Your Latter Is always Greater

At the outset of any project, you will notice that it always appear to be harder. Why? Everything seems daunting during the initial stage. Starting school, writing a book, repairing your home, and building a ministry from ground up all appear difficult when we begin. The negative experiences of today will camouflage the reality of tomorrow. Never judge your future from the point of view of today. In fact, never allow anyone to judge you based on your past or your present situation. As you look ahead, the tasks seem daunting because the entire race lies ahead. The destination appears unreachable, and our goals are seemingly impossible. I remember when my children were quite young, and I would watch them suffer from lack in a variety of ways. I would always quietly say to myself, "I wonder when and if I will ever see them grow up." Looking back now, it's as if they grew up overnight. For the majority of us, life gets better and better as long as we maintain the right attitude and make the right choices as previously mentioned. Moments seem like eternity when things are going wrong. Right now, you may be in a valley experience where it seems like there is no end to the bad news and the pain. But there is always hope that tomorrow will be a better day. Like the personalities listed in Hebrews 11, we must look to the future for a better day and maintain a positive stance, that even if my goals are not accomplished today, the possibility remains that they will come through some time in the future. Faith is defined in the Scriptures as ground or confidence. "Now faith is the substance of things hoped for the evidence of things not seen" (Hebrews 11:1, KJV). While hope is defined as an indication of certainty or a strong and confident expectation. When faith becomes our reality, foundation, or support system, and hope becomes our solid expectation of great things, it is impossible for us to be discouraged. Faith and hope are copartners in helping to create the drive and inspiration to continue the journey, even facing of fears. Most of us boast about faith. We talk about it, preach about it, and study it. However, it becomes a challenge for most of us in reality because we oftentimes do not carry through on what we profess. We are aware that there are levels of faith ranging from saving faith, mustard seed faith, to mature faith. Abraham, the forefather of the Hebrews is described as the father of faith. He stood out in the scriptures as the greatest character of faith because he proactively practiced faith. He did exactly what God commanded him to do and did not deviate from his assignment. Faith then is tangible or real because it affects our behavior in a positive way. When it becomes the driving force of our everyday lives, it propels us into our destiny. Faith also works in agreement with God to perform miracles within the confines of his will. Miracles are events or occurrences that cannot be explained by the laws of nature but can be explained from the Scriptures. God has the authority to override the laws of nature and create special opportunities for his people like the parting of the waters of the River Jordan.

Faith and Hope Are Copartners

On many occasions during the children of Israel's journey, God wrought mighty miracles, supernatural occurrences, in their lives. While the people were genuinely in need of help on all occasions, God needed to prove to them that he really cared for them and was in control of their lives. They, however, took the miracles for granted and became easily dissatisfied as evidenced in their responses to Moses. What an insult to the God who brought them out of Egypt. A spirit of ingratitude was developed very early in the journey. They did not learn to exercise faith and hope along the way. God was looking to build a close relationship. The God of the Hebrews has a nature, personality, and attributes. He feels, hears, listens, gets emotional, and so on. He simply was waiting to interact in an intimate way with his chosen people. There is no difference today. There are times when we find ourselves in crisis, and there is simply no answer or solution to the current circumstances and situations facing us. However, we must bear in mind that every circumstance has a lesson enclosed somewhere in it to be learned. In addition, God permits and allows even negative things to happen in order for us to consult him, engage him, ask him, speak to him, and solicit him for his help. He wants a relationship. On my study of all the major world religions and cults, I noticed a common element running through these religions. Nowhere did they have a god or savior who wanted a personal relationship with those who serve him. Their gods are impersonal, distant, and provide no solution for salvation. Human efforts, according to their doctrines, are necessary for salvation. Today, we have faith in our God that the things that he has promised, he will perform. Jeremiah 29:11 states, "'For I know the thoughts that I think toward you,' saith the LORD, 'thoughts of peace, and not of evil, to give you an expected end'" (KJV). So we have a confident expectation that tomorrow will be a better day. Let us wake up each day and declare the word of God over our lives. God's words increases our faith and gives us hope that we will eventually reach our destination.

Power Points of This Chapter

- The only secret to success is in God.
- No one was born by accident, and therefore, no one should live aimlessly.
- It is the tenacity, determination, and drive that you portray that will in turn serve to provide you with the necessary support you need.
- Your future always looks brighter than today.
- Faith must be your reality and hope your inspiration.

Sinai: A Place of Intimacy with God

> And the Lord said unto Moses, I will do this thing also that thou hast spoken: for thou hast found grace in my sight, and I know thee by name.
>
> Ex. 33:17 (KJV)

Show Me Your Glory

Moses led by example. He was a model leader in every sense of the word. He understood the significance and importance of spending time in the presence of God. He was desperate to know God in an intimate way, so he cried out to God in Exodus chapter two, "Please show me your glory." Moses goal was to broaden his knowledge of God. He wanted to understand the God who interacts with them in a personal way. From a human perspective, he wanted to fear God, understand God, and relate to God. He wanted the people to see that he had a close relationship with the one who they depended upon for their protection, defense, and sustenance. Moses knew the type of followers he had and could not afford to alienate God's presence because every time the people complained and grumbled, God became his support system and encourager. There is nothing as comforting in life than knowing that God is watching your back. There is no problem that is too large for God to address. Many times, in fact quite frequently, I am without answer to the challenges that life brings, but I am confident that he will always show me his glory. Every leader—and we are all leaders in one capacity or another—must know when and how to separate ourselves from the chaos of life and resort to a high place where we can hear and see clearly. Too much time around too many people will cause us to lose focus. Every person has their own way of interpreting experiences, and people never see eye to eye. The children of Israel lived in a camp environment. They were nomads constantly moving from one location to another. That, I believe, created a certain level of unsettling in their spirits. Where there are too many opinions, confusion will develop. Take some time, walk away from the office gossip, leave the environment where the crowd resides, and find rest in the presence of God where he will show you his goodness. Learn to listen to what the people around you have to say, but never be too quick to find answers based on the information they provide you or what they tell you to do. Many people take pleasure in manipulating others; behind the scenes, they will tell you what to do, but publicly they will never take the responsibility. Leaders must be ready to take responsibility for their actions. Knowing that your decisions are made after careful thought and consideration will enable you to make the right choices.

Get Out of the Camp

The crowd has power. There is a level of energy and vibrancy that comes from being in the crowd, particularly in an atmosphere where people are looking for answers and are not exactly sure where they are going. Uncertainty breathes doubt and fear, especially where there is no hope. Everyone needs answers, particularly in a group environment. I see this play out frequently in the church I pastor, when individuals see changes around them and do not know the details. The curious begin to investigate, explore, and seek to find out why they are not moving in the direction they believe, from their point of view, they should be taking. But any wise leader must know that staying in the camp among the noise for too long will tarnish and cloud the vision. There are times when it becomes absolutely necessary to refuse to think like those in the camp. The only way this can be done is to isolate yourself from the camp/crowd and to seek for new absolute truth. The fact that an idea is supported by the majority does not necessarily mean that it is correct. Truth cannot be relative but must be based upon the wisdom from the one who is omniscient, omnipresent, and omnipotent. Sometimes, the most difficult thing to do is to make the decision to step out of our comfort zones into uncharted territories, places where danger and uncertainty lurks. It is, however, in these unexplored places that treasures of opportunities are found.

Is Isolation Necessary?

Isolation is not all bad. There are times when isolation in the form of separation is necessary for survival and posterity. I recall approximately ten years ago when God directed me to resign from the church organization that I was a part of for fifteen years. It was not clear why, but I knew without any doubt that I was making the right decision for my future, as well as the future of the new church I was pastoring. Several pastors I know today have taken a similar route, and their testimonies are generally along the same line. This experience, for me, was horrible because on the one hand, I was separated from the people I love and treasure and on the other hand, my support system was gone. I was unsure which direction to take and became psychologically and emotionally distraught. Unknown to me at the time, it was the plan of God to change my thinking and perspective of who he is and the way he wanted me to do church.

Two years later, after meeting my bishop and pastor, I realized that God needed to remove me from the people I was acquainted with in order to teach and show me that the place where I was, was way too small for me. Indeed when God has great plans for your life, he removes you from the comfort of the crowd, flushes your mind and thinking from the system that trained you to think in a narrow way, and broaden your horizon. Today, I am able to cross denominational lines and cultures to bring the gospel of Jesus Christ to a lost world without the restraints of the doctrines or teachings of a few. It was during my times of separation from the crowd when I ran into the arms of Christ and asked him to teach me his way. I wanted to love my enemies. I wanted to bless those who cursed me. I wanted to live without envy, hate, dislike, and jealousy. I wanted to be free from the chains of sin for real, and I decided that if I was going to be the only one left on the planet that was driven by integrity, it was alright. I found the answer. I found the secret. I found God when I was separated from the crowd. Getting to know God for some initially may be hard work. It is never easy to climb a mountain. Some level of exertion is needed in order to get to the top of the mountain. Seeking and knocking requires commitment, dedication, or faithfulness. You cannot give up after the first attempt. You must move one foot forward in order to get from one point to another. It is more important to find God than to be accepted by the crowd. John Maxwell states, "You must pursue truth over popularity." You will find friends in the crowd, but when crisis begins in your life, very few people will remain with you when the dust settles. Truth will vindicate you, truth will deliver you, and truth will win in the long run. The opinion of people in the majority of instances does not represent the truth. Seek to live a life of truth. You may be lonely in the beginning, but in the end, you will attract the right people.

Climbing the mountain is not easy, but you will discover new possibilities that were never envisioned on the plain. I am a risk taker. It is better to take a risk with a stranger than to live in complacency with the people you are familiar with. Sometimes, life gives us one chance at success, and many people die without taking the risk at the one chance they had for success. It is said that the cemetery is filled with the greatest talents on earth. People die every day without accomplishing because they never take the risk. Walk away from the thinking of the crowd. Walk away from the talking. Walk away from the opinion of the crowd. Sure, it's intimidating and daunting to go against the status quo; sure, you may be filled with apprehension at the thought of being the topic of discussion. But every great leader I know exposed themselves to become the topic of debate. We must become resilient against criticisms and harden ourselves and be ready to become exposed as we climb to the top of Sinai. Sinai is a part of the journey, and it represents the opportunities that come your way wherein you may see the glory of God. Everyone has a moment in time when a door is opened to them. According to Bishop T. D. Jakes, we must "maximize the moment." I could not afford to miss my moment. I was wise enough to recognize that moment, and I grabbed it, lost some friends in the moment but at the outcome, gained new lifelong friends.

Are You a Friend of God?

Become a friend of God; let him know you by your name. In his presence, there is joy and peace. When you pray, after you say what you believe, you must say to yourself, "Stop, stop, stop!" and then listen to the voice of God. Never forget that he speaks. Long prayers are popular. For some reason, we believe that the longer we pray, the more results we get. The more mature I become spiritually and the closer I get to God, I have come to the realization that long prayers are not absolutely necessary. It is our posture, our heart, and our mindset that matters. We are admonished to pray without ceasing, and that does not necessarily entail praying nonstop for hours. I find that, for me, praying without ceasing is having my mind and heart in tune with God to the point where I listen to what he has to say. I, however, cherish those times when I am able to spend hours in his presence, just us, no noise, and no people.

During Adam's reign in the Garden of Eden, God developed a simple system where each day they would spend time together. The garden was not crowded with people, technology, stuff, noise, and the stress we deal with every day. It was a place of work but also a place where God met man in the cool of the day. Notice that every day, there was interaction between Adam and God. According to the Scriptures, it was not God that caused the separation; it was the disobedience of man. God continued to search for man while man was hiding. After the Eden story, God continued to make efforts to this day to restore his relationship with man. God wants to be our friend. How can we accomplish this? Restoring a relationship built upon obedience and submission to his plan for our lives will accomplish the task. According to John Bevere, "People say, 'God is my friend. He understands my heart.'" It is true that God does understand our hearts even more thoroughly than we can understand ourselves. But usually, this comment is given in the justification of actions that contradict his covenant. The fact is they are in disobedience to God's Word. In the Scriptures, the only people I see God calling his friends are those who tremble at his word and presence and are quick to obey no matter the cost."

Excellence Built in Isolation

I admire individuals who do not settle for less. Mediocrity is a breeding ground for failure. A spirit of excellence, if fostered, will bring results that are far-reaching. Some of the greatest breakthroughs in science and technology are not made in the loud office spaces but within the confines of a small isolated room. Some of the greatest ministries are birthed out from people who experienced social isolation and deprivation of one kind or another. I am always fascinated with the stories of important people with humble beginnings. One example is my spiritual father who has become a world renowned religious leader in a continent where in recent years, spiritual darkness abounds. On many of my trips to England, I would just sit in my bishop's church and observe the order of service. They appear to have it down to a science. The ushers, the choir, the clergy all look distinguished, dressed in their well-coordinated attire. I noticed on my first visit that the choir members literally smiled while singing in addition to their polished look. I thought the church I pastor, (a little less formal) needed to be like this one. I proactively took back and implemented many of the things I saw with much success. Wherever there is excellence, seek to learn and implement those systems and processes that will improve your organization. So Sinai is a place of separation, silence, submission, and isolation, but of most significance, it's the place where God spoke to Moses face to face. When we find a place in God where we see him for ourselves, we will never return to the crowd the way we left. People will see the change in you because the presence of God glows. It is this place where we develop a level of commitment that surpasses that of the camp people. Covenants are made on Sinai, revelations are received on Sinai, partnerships are built on Sinai, and the past—the hidden things of God are revealed on Sinai. We cannot dismiss this portion of the journey. We can circle the mountain and stay in the camp or climb the mountain. Let's choose to separate ourselves from the crowd and climb the mountain. New discoveries await us in his presence.

Every visionary will tell you that it was in their quiet moments with God when they received the vision to plan their destinies. Most books are written in the silence of homes, office spaces, and nature; most leaders received their training during periods when they were left alone with no other voice but the voice of God to hear.

Power Points of This Chapter

- Too much time around too many people will cause us to lose focus.
- You will find friends in the crowd, but when crisis begin in your life, very few people will remain with you when the dust settles.
- Wherever there is excellence, seek to learn and implement those systems and processes that will improve your organization.

Jordan: Barrier or Opportunity

> Remember the word which Moses the servant of the lord commanded you, saying, The Lord your God is giving you rest and is giving you this land.
>
> Joshua 1:13 (KJV)

So you are getting older, and you feel disappointed that for years, the majority of your personal dreams have not yet come to pass. You are still struggling with a sense of failure because you have not completed college. You have not received the marriage proposal you expected. You have not had children nor landed the job or promotion you expected. Well, recently, I informed a group of people that age is only a number. What matters more is that you put the past behind you and ask God to give you a plan for the rest of your life. I have seen people in their sixties, seventies, and even their eighties live their lives with excitement by returning to school, finding fulfillment in giving back to their communities, and starting new projects that create new opportunities. Going around in circles for years can deplete you of your energy to the point where you decide to stop trying and simply give up. But waiting is not all that bad. Most of us do not like the word "wait," but important things will not be released into your hands until you have the level of maturity to handle the responsibility. God's glory is heavy; it comes with responsibility and accountability. It will not be poured out upon individuals who are not ready mentally, emotionally, and physically.

When the Going Gets Tough

There is a price for fame, and there is a price for success. Every stage in your life is accompanied by laughter and tears. The good times parallel the bad times, and many people who arrive at their destination too quickly oftentimes embarrass themselves and their family. They forget how they got there and mismanage success because of lack of preparation. Immaturity will create circles in your life, and God will make you wait until you are grown up to give you the desires of your heart. In fact, immaturity can abort the great things you desire. Maintaining the right attitude in life by demonstrating humility and obedience speak volumes about where we are headed. I remember the first professional position I held as a librarian. I consistently showed up on time for work and exercised discipline in all aspects of my job responsibility. I was proactive but gave full support to my boss by filling in when the need arose, working extra time when I was needed, and simply went above and beyond the call of duty to perform well. Needless to say, when the time came for a promotion, I was quickly recommended for the position. I am the executive director of the company today after starting at the bottom. I worked my way upwards by maintaining the right attitude.

At twelve years old, I made a decision that I would become a doctor one day. I desired to have a doctorate degree, and during the course of my life, I never allowed my dream to die. On occasions, I would set my goals for five years or so and included that portion of my dream into my plans. At age forty, I applied to two major universities to complete my degree. At the point of beginning a program at a prestigious college, I was called into ministry to become a pastor. I was told clearly to postpone this plan. Twelve years later, I graduated with my doctorate in theology and not public administration as planned. God tweaked my plans and gave me the opportunity to pursue the path that he planned for me. My life today is no longer about me; it is lived on purpose. Every decision is made prayerfully and consciously within the confines of God's plan. The waiting was worth it. Achieving greatness too early can become a detriment to us rather than a benefit. I am grateful for the opportunity and the courage I had to wait. Remember, God has a plan for your life, and since he plans it from the point of view of eternity, he knows best when to bring things into time. Timing is important.

The group that left Israel, up to this point, changed significantly demographically. Forty years had expired, and Israel had not reached their destination. Children were born and became parents. Older people died, and young people matured. Time can erode memories of the past; time can change attitude and opinion and force us to grow up and take on new responsibilities. For Israel, forty years of wandering successfully changed the ability of some; Joshua was ready for a new leadership role for sure. The people correspondingly needed a change in leadership. The people perfected the art of grumbling and demonstrated behavior patterns that were inconsistent with the character of God. However, a promise was made to them, and God was determined to bring them into their place of promise. So at this point, Moses was dead and buried by God. A brilliant leader with tremendous diplomatic skills was gone. Israel was in mourning, and both Joshua and the people were in a state of grief and depression. How can God ask me to arise and move when I am experiencing the worst time of my life? Someone may say, "He needs to speak when I am happy and have everything going well for me. But no, he spoke right at the worst possible time." Joshua was told to arise and go over Jordan. It is paramount for us to understand that our destiny is sometimes camouflaged in crisis. The concept of the tipping point could be applied here. Gladwell defines a tipping point as "the moment of critical mass, the threshold, the boiling point." Societies and cultures are changed dramatically by one small thing or a few persons with the right abilities. Israel could either dissolve as a nation here, or they could refocus, regroup, become motivated and energized, and utilize this social dilemma to mobilize the people and get them into the promise land. This very negative situation could be turned into positive with the right leader having the right skill sets at the right time. Moses's successor was Joshua who was chosen by God. This was the person with the right skill sets for the right moment. What was needed for this season was a brilliant warrior and strategist in warfare. Joshua was bold, energetic, and aggressive. He was never afraid of the enemy, and he confronted the laziness of the people as the commander in chief. He had no patience for complaints, and unlike Moses, he was not prepared to ask God for a miracle to feed the people neither for anything for them to drink. Hard work and warfare was his strategy. He was the right person chosen at the right time. At some point in the journey, we may need to change and expand our abilities. We may need to develop and utilize new skills. In other words, we may need to reinvent ourselves. Sometimes, a new career and a whole new mindset may be required to accomplish great things.

The Spirit of Joshua

Joshua accepted the challenge, followed directives, and ended forty years of wilderness experience. The choice they made was to gather up the pieces, energize, and mobilize the entire community and move into a period of conquest and possession of the land. That required physical, mental, and creative skills all at the same time. Jordan was no longer a barrier. It became their open door. The things that sometimes appear daunting and intimidating can become stepping-stones when we change our outlook. Everyone was united with a new set of goals as they approached their promise. Notice there was no time for complaining. A period of conquest awaits them, and the idea of milk and honey, planting and reaping their own food encouraged them along. They had a new vision; to settle the land and the mission was to remove all obstacles out of their way. They knew that they had to fight, but they were ready for the new challenges. I read a book once entitled Managing Energy And Not Time. The premise was that rather than managing time by allocating tasks to our day or schedule, we should manage energy. By managing the latter, we are able to devote high energy periods to the most difficult tasks. Those tasks that require less energy may be done at our low energy period. Our overall effort and success rate will be greater in the long run. Israel at this time was managing energy. They utilized daytime hours and the people with the appropriate abilities for the task. Those with spiritual responsibilities focused on their tasks, while the warriors/soldiers accomplished their assignments. Teamwork was instituted, and under God's directive, they were able to cross the Jordan. One leader took them to the brink, and another brought them through and over. Two completely different resumes were placed on the table for the two significant time periods. The phase of the journey from Egypt to the end of the wilderness demanded the abilities of Moses. The last phase of the journey did not require a leader with great diplomatic skills; it required a valiant, fearless leader who would look the enemy dead in his eyes and say, "Whose side are you on?" Crossing Jordan demands a new mode of conduct and a team who will forget the experiences of Egypt. This new group was delivered mentally and emotionally from bondage and was ready and prepared to enter into their destiny. They were driven by the spirit of Joshua. A new level of motivation pervaded the camp as the people received a glimpse of the place of promise where they would find rest from the wandering. Do you feel as if you are right on the brink of the greatest breakthrough in your life? Then you probably are. Adapt the confidence of Joshua, and with an assertive attitude, move forward with your plans to accomplish the impossible.

Power Points of This Chapter

- Every stage in your life is accompanied by laughter and tears.
- Immaturity will create circles in your life, and God will make you wait until you are grown up to give you the desires of your heart.
- We may need to reinvent ourselves.
- The things that sometimes appear daunting and intimidating can become stepping-stones when we change our outlook.

Jericho: Bringing Down the Walls

> "And the Lord said to Joshua: See I have given Jericho into your hand, its King and the mighty men of valor."
>
> Joshua 6:2 (KJV)

If You Can Use Anything, Lord, You Can Use Me

It is evident from Scriptures that God has a record of using people who are lacking in professional skills and business acumen. Moses had a speech impediment. Gideon had no professional and military training. Samson had major social and emotional weaknesses. Paul was a murderer. David was an adulterer, and the list goes on. In addition, the methods of warfare that are sometimes employed by God to deliver us are unconventional to the point of weird. You need not come to the table prepared with your gifts, experiences, and training. If you are selected as the candidate to be used by God for a project, mission, or assignment, your responsibility is simply to trust and obey. You will notice that as time progresses, you will either develop or demonstrate new abilities that you thought you were not capable of exhibiting, or you will be given favor and grace to make it happen. Recently, a visiting pastor at my church shared a quotation he heard from a public speaker, and I paraphrase it as: You put an egg into hot water, it cracks; you put a tea bag into hot water, it changes the color and context of the water. We should be like the tea bag; you never know how strong it is until it's placed in hot water. The water doesn't change the tea bag, but the teabag changes the water. God wants to use you; yes, despite the long list of negatives. Since the credit must be given to God only, he will ensure that every battle is won at the right time. It is more exciting to win the war than the battle. So wherever you are at this time and whatever you are experiencing, you will never lose when God fights. He fights one battle at a time until you progressively and ultimately win the war. Jericho was a great, huge, giant wall that stood in the path of the people's destiny. It was intimidating and was meant to be a distraction and a discouragement. Yet the people followed the command to march around it six times and to shout at the seventh time. If you know anything about science, warfare, and military strategy, you will understand that this did not make sense. The walls, however, came tumbling down as the story goes. This phase of the journey demands that you work with God and agree with him even though it may sound ridiculous.

My most recent Jericho came in the form of a giant building that was placed on the market. As previously mentioned, it was simply an impossible venture from every angle. We needed approximately two million dollars for down payment and repairs, and in addition, we must seek approval from the village to purchase one of the largest buildings on its tax roll. From the outset, we knew two things: we needed the building, and it was pointed out to us by God. After months of being frustrated because we were under pressure to move out from our rented space located in the backroom of a small local church, I attended a conference where my bishop was scheduled to be the main speaker. This message propelled my faith to a level I have never experienced before. My bishop preached from the story of the Prophet Elisha when he commanded the king to strike again until the enemy is totally destroyed. My bishop announced that God would release his blessings on those who believe his word. Out of sheer desperation from being frustrated, I did the ridiculous. I extended my faith like never before and declared to my church on my return that within thirty days, something must happen. After five days, I was driving by a building and very clearly, I heard the voice of God said, "Call that number." I responded. The sign indicated "space for lease" and not for sale. Moreover, that property was listed three years ago for three million dollars. Finally, I decided to call the church's realtor. The gentleman responded, "Pastor Joan that building is absolutely not for sale." The real estate office was across from the building, and its staff was fully acquainted with the listed commercial properties in town. I insisted, and the agent promised that he would make the call to investigate. The next day, the phone call came. The agent was beaming through the phone. He announced I have good news. The owner would like to sell the property to the church. That one phone call changed my life and our ministry for good. Three years of marching around the wall of Jericho began when we started the process of acquiring approval from the Zoning Board, Planning Board, and Building Department, seeking a mortgage and renovating this thirty-four thousand-square foot facility. The wall was broken down one piece at a time, and the impossible happened. We had exactly enough funds for our closing and exactly enough funds for our renovation. We learned to pray like never before, trusted God like never before, and invested everything we had into this venture. Today, we are in that place of promise, and as we reflect on the experiences, it was indeed merely a part of the journey.

The Weapons of Your Warfare Are Not Carnal

Maintain your integrity at any cost. Never compromise your values. Hold on to the principles that you were taught in the Word of God. Too many people, especially leaders are failing because they are unable to say no to the flesh and the attractions that the kingdom of the world presents. Every individual will be tested at some point in their life. During our season of testing we cannot forget that believers do not play by the rules of the world. The truth is not relative, but rather, it is dictated to us by God in his word. God established a relationship at the outset with the Hebrews that created a system whereby God would fight their battles for them. Each time they encountered an enemy, before a decision was made in terms of how to respond, they consulted God. There was never an approach that was not solidified and confirmed by God. For Moses, that was a basic rule, and indeed for Joshua, the same rule applied. On rare occasions, when this system was not followed precisely, it ended in disaster. During these times, the leader and people repented and returned to follow the right approach. They proved in innumerable ways that it was the hand of God that prevailed and not their personal strength and gifting. In fact, the majority of times, they were outnumbered when compared with the enemy. We must understand that God is the best at what he does. He will never fail at any attempt to fight for us. I have personally experienced victory over and over after consulting God and turning over my challenges to him. It is brilliant how we can observe the corrective hands of God in terms of the way he maneuvers unfair circumstances on our behalf. We will always win in the long run as long as we maintain the right attitude and take the high road.

Forgiveness as a Weapon

Your enemies will fight with weapons that the Bible describes as carnal, but you must not. Be quick to forgive and slow to become angry. I shared with my colleagues recently that one of the most powerful tools I utilize to succeed and remain happy is the weapon of forgiveness. Rather than retaliating or responding immediately, I remove myself from the scene of the conflict or incident and think, pray, and reflect before I speak. I have consistently and proactively ensured that anyone who has hurt me in any way, whether a family member, a colleague, or someone in the church, I will forgive quickly. Becoming bitter about unfair treatment will result in serious consequences. I mentioned earlier that along my journey, I was married at an early age, straight out of high school. I neglect to share my story in any detail; however, it was painful. I remained faithful despite the fact that I was abandoned and left with three children on my own to parent. Countless people experience the same tragedy of abandonment and divorce. For those like me who would never initiate a separation and dissolution of marriage, it is even harder. However, it is critical that I remove all bitterness and forgive completely for my own spiritual and emotional health. I survived the ordeal and am enjoying life to the fullest because of the decision I made to put the past behind me and look to the promise that God has prepared for me.

The Spoken and Written Word as a Weapon

Death and life are in the power of the tongue.

Proverbs 18:21 (KJV)

Words are effective in either a positive or negative way. I have learned that words are weapons and if carelessly used, will create permanent damage. Words are irretrievable weapons and sometimes "sorry" does not work. Aim to speak positive words over yourself, your family, and people in general. Remove yourself from negative speaking and from people who engage in negative conversations, particularly those conversations concerning people's private affairs. It is critical that we think before we speak and become responsible communicators. In my lifetime, the words I listen and read have transformed my life in innumerable ways. During times when I am lonely, demotivated, and discouraged, the words of my friends, strangers, pastor, and colleagues have served to revive, motivate, and encourage me. There is no word as powerful as the word of God. It is in the Bible that I find solace, comfort, encouragement, peace, joy, fulfillment, and purpose by simply opening the pages and reading the Word. The spoken word from great preachers that are renowned in America, such as Bishop John Francis, Joyce Myers, Bishop T.D. Jakes, and Pastor Jackie McCullough has served to change my life from one of mediocrity to that of excellence. I have been motivated, challenged, and mentored indirectly by their stories, thinking, resilience, commitment, and dedication to Christian values. I have spent countless hours listening to their presentation on particular subjects that speak to my need and my destiny. It is upon their lives that I have built mine. I have no desire to duplicate their experiences or to become a photocopy of these great people. However, their stories have helped me to find my place and to become who God wants me to be, as a unique person. Today, I have overcome every adversity that life has brought my way, and now I am in my place of promise. It happened only recently, so I am yet to see the greatest days of my life. I have now started my own journey to give back to the world that has given me so much through the written and spoken word. As a librarian, I am exposed to the written word every day and can attest to the value and power of it. On occasions, children I encouraged to read through story times, reading programs, and the variety of initiatives and activities I utilized over the years to promote reading would return after graduating from college to say thanks. I have observed children maturing from barely having the ability to pronounce words to graduating with a master's degree. It is remarkable how reading can frame the thinking, educate, and empower people to make the right choices. Knowledge is truly power, and it's a disservice to God not to take time to read critically. Every book or information presented must be carefully examined for its authenticity because people write with all types of motives, and unfortunately, reading the wrong material and believing its contents can be detrimental. Nevertheless, there is power in reading; understanding what you read, learning from what you read, and living what you read can transform your life. Read books written and recommended by someone you trust and respect. Read books reviewed by writers and professionals who are well respected, not necessarily by people who are famous. Some of the worst role models for our children are those who are classified as famous in our world. My role models are people with integrity, longevity, and who have impacted and changed our world for good. What are you reading today at this phase of the journey?

Self-discipline as a Weapon

Self-discipline is a counter weapon that may be used effectively against the enemy. Self-discipline can be defined as the ability to motivate oneself in spite of a negative emotional state. Qualities associated with self-discipline include willpower, hard work, and persistence. A disciplined person will not be controlled by emotions and feelings but will keep moving forward, even in the face of fears. He will not be easily discouraged but rather is driven and is forward-thinking. The belief of a disciplined person is that tomorrow will be better than today. An individual who knows how to exercise self-control, particularly during difficult times will win the battle. In my lifetime, I have observed too many adults who have absolutely no control over their emotions, attitudes, and behavior. They act and speak without thinking and stop only after they react inappropriately. These people are generally not successful. They are never at peace, and they wander around the mountain of their life and never seem to leave their wilderness experience. It is consistent good behavior that brings positive results. The hallmark of success is faithfulness. This is a decision everyone must make, that they will not be controlled by events and circumstances but rather will be in control. Some that I have counseled do not regard the opinion of friends, colleagues, or even the Word of God. Their attitudes are determined by their own opinion and feelings. But a mature person will always be in control of their speech and behavior. It amazes me when I observe older people who behave like children without giving consideration to the impact this has on the people they interact with on a daily basis. We must remember that we do not live for ourselves but for others, and every decision, attitude, and behavior pattern has consequences both for ourselves and for others. We must aim to command respect from others by giving respect first.

Laughter as a Weapon

I recently preached a sermon entitled "God Is Going to Make You Laugh." Laughter is a weapon that we underestimate. It is considered a weapon against suffering and despair. I once heard that laughter could be a weapon against suffering and can help us to make it through traumatic situations. This expectation serves two vitally important functions. It diminishes, or even eliminates, the moment-by-moment suffering we might otherwise experience as a result of a traumatic loss, which actually makes it more likely we will make it through the trauma unmarred and flourish once again. Laughter, then in crisis, creates the expectation that it will be alright and that things are not as bad as they may appear. People sometimes think it's inappropriate to laugh during crisis, as I find myself doing frequently these days. This weapon, I believe, is underutilized because it is a means by which we all can encourage ourselves during times of adversity.

When faced with sickness, misfortune, pain, and bad news, laugh at the situation, laugh at the circumstances. Rather than permitting fear, loneliness, doubt, and the array of negative emotions to consume you, laugh. People may not necessarily appreciate your response, but it's better to have someone annoyed with you than allow fear to consume your life. You have one shot at life, one opportunity, and you cannot afford to die from depression, sadness, and dismay. Laughter will deliver you from sadness and divert your attention from the incident or situation. It will diminish the negative impact that would otherwise result from the event or experience.

One late afternoon, I was driving home as usual from my office after an uneventful day. I was looking forward to being home this particular evening because it was late spring and my schedule was free for the evening. Working as a senior pastor and as a library director keep me quite busy, along with the multitude of other responsibilities. Over the years, I have adopted five young ladies who all became an intricate part of my life. Five minutes away from my home, I received an urgent phone call from one of my daughters. The fear came almost literally through the telephone as she proceeded to advise me that her birth mother, who lives fifteen minutes from my home, fainted and is unconscious. She further elaborated that her older sister visited the scene and also fainted on noticing the condition of her mother. My daughter continued to describe the scene with the ambulances, the people, everyone's reaction, and the preceding events that climaxed into this horrible moment. Without thinking, out of somewhere in my subconscious came laughter. I gave no thought to my response, neither did I understand why but the words came out like this: "Please ensure that you do not pass out as well because that would be three of you." Of course, I was lovingly reprimanded for my response. I now know that an innate defense system kicked in, in the form of laughter. I survived the moment, stopped at my house to prepare to meet my daughter at the hospital, and in five minutes, I received the call. It was the worst. A massive brain aneurism took the life of this woman who was exactly my age. It has been proven that laughter encourages friendship and socialization because it takes two or more people, on most occasions, to generate laughter. There is generally an initiator, the person who makes a statement verbally or otherwise that stimulates laughter. Notice, anyone who suffers from depression generally does not laugh and removes himself from the environment where there is laughter and socialization. For unknown reasons, humor stimulates your creativity and overall makes you feel better about everything. Never allow the stops in your journey to remove your laughter. I recently spoke to a group of individuals on the subject, and I took the liberty to make the point that on occasions when I cry for prolonged period of time concerning an event or situation, I seem to lose the ability to think creatively. Notice that crying generally isolates you from the people who genuinely care, you hold down your head, desire to be alone, and during the process, you do not think rationally, speak rationally, or even act rationally. According to the writer of Ecclesiastes 3:1-10 (KJV):

> To every thing there is a season, and a time to every purpose under the heaven:
>   A time to be born, and a time to die; a time to plant, and a time to pluck up that which is planted;
>   A time to kill, and a time to heal; a time to break down, and a time to build up;
>   A time to weep, and a time to laugh; a time to mourn, and a time to dance;

> A time to cast away stones, and a time to gather stones together; a time to embrace, and a time to refrain from embracing;
>
> A time to get, and a time to lose; a time to keep, and a time to cast away;
>
> A time to rend, and a time to sew; a time to keep silence, and a time to speak;
>
> A time to love, and a time to hate; a time of war, and a time of peace.
>
> What profit hath he that worketh in that wherein he laboureth?
>
> I have seen the travail, which God hath given to the sons of men to be exercised in it.

Never allow anyone or anything to steal your time to laugh. You have left your Egypt, wandered in the wilderness with your promise, and now, it is your time to laugh. Everyone has their time when your opportunities for greatness manifest. Well, celebrate with laughter, and even when you are faced with crisis, seek to laugh at everything. Laugh at yourself, make light of every situation, and you will enjoy the journey. Agree with the scriptures:

> A joyful heart is good medicine, but a crushed spirit dries up the bones.
>
> Proverbs 17:22 (KJV)

Laughter is intricately connected to your faith. People who are mature in faith can laugh at their problems, and even their weaknesses. Leaders who can make light of negative events and joke at themselves are mature. Those who allow people to poke fun at them are often mature in their attitude and behavior. Keep laughing.

Power Points of This Chapter

- You will notice that as time progress, you will either develop or demonstrate new abilities that you thought you were not capable of exhibiting or you will be given favor and grace to make it happen.
- The hallmark of success is faithfulness.
- When faced with sickness, misfortune, pain, and bad news, laugh at the situation, laugh at the circumstances. Rather than permitting fear, loneliness, doubt, and the array of negative emotions to consume you, laugh.

PART 3

IN THE PROMISE LAND

Taking Territories

> Now the man Moses was more humble, more than all men who were on the face of the earth.
>
> Numbers 12:3 (KJV)

Moses: A Glimpse of the Promise

Moses was called by God when he was eighty years old. Through the experience of the burning bush, his life was changed forever by this one encounter with the one true God. Moses was educated in the courts of Pharaoh as an adopted child. He was highly trained in Egyptian politics and culture. Since he was Hebrew and became aware of his ancestry at an early age, I am sure that, like anyone else, he explored his ancestry, learned their experiences, and understood the nature of their enslavement. Moses was exposed to the best food, clothing, housing, education, and people of importance and affluence. He ran away after taking sides with one of his own, a Hebrew, when he witnessed their abuse firsthand. He became a murderer and a wanted man in Egypt and ran to escape the possible consequences of his behavior. But here he was, at this point in his life, living in the desert tending sheep, a profession for the poor in Egypt. He lived on the mountainside day after day for forty long years with the same monotony. He would wake up tending sheep and defending sheep and would go to bed tending sheep, only to wake up the next day to begin the cycle again. That was faithfulness. From time to time, he must have wondered what was happening in the courts of Pharaoh and more importantly among his own people. He was not only separated from his own culture but was also separated from the people and culture of his adopted family. He was living in a strange place with strange people and strange animals with a strange profession. Unbeknownst to Moses, God had a major plan for his life, and he was simply in training for one of the greatest projects on the planet. One that would not only impact and affect a small race of people but one that would have great consequences for the rest of the world. In this small isolated place, God visited Moses and introduced himself to him as the I Am That I Am.

History has proven that God has chosen those of us with very little influence, money, social standing, and political power and use us to change the world. Moses was no exception; like me, I was at the worst point in my life when God visited and popped the question.

"There is a Macedonian call in Ossining, New York. Can you go preach the gospel?" God visited Moses, introduced himself, and gave him the assignment of a promise keeper. According to Os Hillman, "Life is often seen backward." Many times, we do not understand the ways of God until we have passed through the valleys and can stand upon the mountaintop and see the path behind us. Only then can we appreciate why this or that lesson was required in our process. For Moses, it was absolutely necessary for him to be raised in the courts of Pharaoh, to understand their custom, their ways, and how they thought. Who better to bring a people out of Egyptian slavery than who has been on the other side of the fence as a slave lord?

Sure, there was destiny on Moses's life because he was slated to be killed at birth when Pharaoh became concerned about the volume of male children that were populating the country of Egypt and decided that the best birth control measure was to massacre all Hebrew male newborns. The midwives chosen for the job were acquainted with God and decided not to fulfill the desires of the king. Moses life was spared because of the refusal of these midwives to support this wicked act. They made a choice to continue to deliver these Hebrew babies and suffer the consequences if caught rather than obeying the voice of a man. In the process, they saved the greatest deliverer and lawgiver the world has ever witnessed. Out of the hands of these fearless women came Moses. God must have acted in mercy in part based on the attitude of these female radicals. According to John Maxwell, "At a strange junction in history, these Hebrew midwives – politically powerless, socially despised, economically disadvantaged- defied the ruler of Egypt to obey the God they feared. Their perilous choice to do the right thing protected the line of Abraham through which the Messiah would come, thus fulfilling God's plan for not only the Hebrew, but for all mankind."

Pharaoh had power but no character, wisdom, nor integrity. For self-preservation and self-protection, he decided the best and only way was to commit genocide.

Remove the threat he thought, and his confidence as a leader would not be eroded. So the pressure was placed upon the Hebrew slaves to work harder, work longer hours, increase their burden, and finally to murder their babies. He failed because the right behavior, truth, and integrity will win in the long run. God preserved the life of Moses, permitted him to enter into the courts of the king for training and experience, then again permitted him to gain experience for forty years in a harsh, lonely, and difficult environment. Forty years within the courts of the king and forty years in the wilderness was adequate experience. The entire process was engineered by God. Maxwell states, "How did God prepare Moses to be His man to lead the Hebrews out of Egyptian bondage? He prepared him not in a day, but over time; not through an event, but with a process. Of course, others before Moses waited years for God to fulfill His leadership development process:

- Noah waited 120 years before the predicted rains arrive.
- Abraham waited 25 years for a promised son.
- Joseph waited 14 years in prison for a crime he didn't commit.
- Job waited perhaps a lifetime, 6–70 years, for God's justice."

Does this sound familiar to you as it relates to your personal life journey? For me, it resonates perfectly. I was informed that at approximately age two, I died, and funeral arrangements were being made when suddenly I woke up from my unconscious state at the end of the day. I recall a childhood of much sickness. I mentioned earlier that my mother died at childbirth when I was at the age of four. I was the last child of nine siblings. I grew up as a tomboy and remember wearing shoes on a regular basis when I turned twelve years old. Looking back, I am not sure how I survived my exciting childhood, which was spent outdoors climbing trees, running through cow pastures, and engaging in the multitude of dangerous activities, growing up. I later endured rejection, divorce, isolation, envy, jealousy, a broken heart, and the list goes on, but I have endured it all. Today, I have a glimpse of the promise.

Moses was given a glimpse of the promise. God gave Moses the vision of where they were headed before the people even understood what lies ahead of them. He was humble, diplomatic, obedient, determined, and committed to the cause. He was vigilant in obtaining information from God, acted as he heard God, and moved accordingly. God acted on the foundation that was already laid in the life of Moses and provided the necessary moral support he needed. We all need a few good people around us to function as our support system as we engineer the path God has created for us. Moses had his father-in-law, Jethro, first, followed by Aaron. Help came in stages and as needed. Important people were placed in his life during the initial stage of the journey until the end. We should never depend on the crowd to believe in the vision because someone from the crowd, sooner or later, will challenge what God has started. Moses's support system consisted of very few people. His inner circle consisted of the minority, but it was those whom God chose to fill the need that mattered. Most people who are popular are generally lonely because when the lights are turned off and they go home, reality sets in, and it's the opinion of those who are closest that really matters.

The following important things contributed to Moses longevity as a leader:

- Moses had the necessary background, training, and experience to lead.
- Moses was a Hebrew; he could identify with the people and the cause.
- Moses had a support system from start to finish—Jethro, Aaron, and Joshua.
- Moses consulted God before he made any decision. He never acted independently.
- Moses had mentors.
- Moses learned to respect both the easy life and the hard life.
- Moses was driven by vision and mission.
- God's presence never left Moses.

The above factors contributed in molding the character of Moses as a great leader. Along with his personality and life experiences, he became one of the greatest leaders ever lived because he knew who he was and depended upon God completely for sustenance and survival. You and I are no exception to the rule if we desire to be used by God in a remarkable way. Moses's journey with the Hebrews must be looked upon with respect and for our learning. Since the nature of the God of the Old Testament does not change, there is something special and remarkable about the journey that is documented for our learning. We must understand that our unique personality, experiences, background, and training can be used by God for the greater good. The people in our lives who provide leadership, mentorship, and support must be respected and treasured. Never take anyone or anything for granted. The presence of God in your life is paramount to your success, and you will never get to your place of promise without him. And finally, you must develop a personal strategic plan for your life. Vision will give you focus because you will know where you are going, and your mission will motivate you to wake up every day and keep moving. I have yet to see a believer reach their destination—the zenith of their spiritual walk—without the hands of God on their lives. St. Paul declared, "I have fought a good fight. I have kept the faith. I have finished the course, and henceforth, is laid up for me a crown of righteousness and not for me only but for all those who wait for his appearing."

I pause here to share another testimony about the unfailing goodness of God. My soul mate growing up was my late cousin George Sewell. We decided at age twelve that we would become doctors one day. No one told us about careers or professions. There were no mentors that sat us down and taught us about life and what to expect. We saw our grandmother reading the family Bible, went to church, attended school, and joined the local Book Mobile. There was neither television nor electricity in my village until I was about thirteen years old. Probably through reading and attending public school, we decided that we wanted to become doctors. During tenth grade in high school, my cousin migrated to Canada. My heart was broken, but I continued to remain focused on completing high school and graduating. My cousin in Canada graduated from high school and went straight into college to pursue his life's dream. I graduated and started a family. Our communication became less and less over the years until we reconnected after graduating from college. He enjoyed his college life and quickly became a doctor. The mistake was he forgot God in the process. I struggled through community college, then through university, and continued to graduate school with very little resources. Along the way, I was always thanking and giving credit to the hands of God upon my life. I remained relatively committed to Christ, even during times when I did not attend church while in school. Finally, I reconnected with my cousin after migrating to the United States and was shocked to learn quickly that he no longer believed in God. During one of our conversations, I was boldly asked why I go to church since it's my job that pays my bills. Every conversation surrounded money, power, fame, and how much we have accomplished by attending college. Our relationship sadly ended when my cousin was diagnosed with terminal cancer and died at age forty. This event changed my life forever. I knew then that I must live on purpose. I must encourage those who I lead that life is much more than material possession. I knew deep down in my heart that I did not want to accomplish so much yet so little. I wanted to pour myself into individuals and empower them to know that they can reach their place of promise and that God is the driving force that propels us into our destiny. You and I, as Pastor Rick Warren states, "were born for a purpose" and must live on purpose every phase of the journey. There is purpose in every stop we make.

Standard in the Workplace

Every believer and indeed every person must set personal standards in order to make a difference. Many of us, at our place of employment, are probably the only person who our colleagues will come to know Christ through. Rather than being embarrassed about our faith, we must let them see that we are different and that we have something greater to offer. We must take the principles of God with us to the office environment. We must take the presence of God with us to the world through the doors of the marketplace rather than leaving our Christian lifestyle in the parking lot. I know there is a reason why I am not released from my job. I continue to work because that season of my life is not over. There is a reason, a purpose why millions of Christians are placed in the same office space with someone who is not acquainted with our God. Every human being has a god—something that drives them—whether it is their education, profession, family, possessions, etc., there is a reason for living. In addition, everyone is searching for a reason why they exist. Everyone is searching for the secret to their existence. Everyone I know wants to make a difference. We have a responsibility to share our faith in a God that rules the universe directly or indirectly. There is a sense of urgency for every Christian believer to arise, mobilize themselves, and see the confusion of the world. The explosion in technology, deterioration in morality, famine, slavery, and the multitude of negative forces coming against our families makes it necessary to fight back. We must fight back with the truth, we must fight back with honesty and integrity, and we must fight back in every corner of the world, especially those places where we spend our waking hours.

God can use us anywhere to make a difference. Whenever and wherever we are, we can announce the goodness of God. Our vocation can become an instrument to bring glory to God. While interacting with the people we spend so much time with on a daily basis, we can demonstrate love, forgiveness, joy, peace, long-suffering, meekness, self-control, and faith right in their presence. Those are the fruits of the Spirit. While they may see and observe our weaknesses, they can also see the values we carry. Unknowingly, we can all be changing lives around us every day. We must be strategic and deliberate in our endeavor to change the world. Os Hillman gave the following list as some of the reasons why God creates work:

1. We work to meet human needs
2. He wanted us to view our work as ministry
3. We are to view our work as worship to God
4. We are to use our work as a platform to share the love of God
5. We work to earn money to fund God's work on the earth

6. We work to care for the poor
7. We work to transform culture
8. We work to bring glory to God

Work generally prepares us for our spiritual assignments. The location of our assignments may be right at our workplace or at some future distant place. Either way, God values work and uses it to enhance his kingdom's purpose.

Standard in the Home

Homes, to a great extent, have become war zones for many families rather than a place of relaxation, peace, and enjoyment. God's high standards are applicable to the home. We must become stewards in the home and create loving, happy families. I write on behalf of the thousands of homes without a father. I have experienced both sides of the fence. I know what it means to have a family with both parents living at home, and I also know what it means to be a single parent. Each comes with its own set of challenges. A single family has challenges just as much as a family headed by both parents. Oh, how critical it is for a father and husband to maintain God's standards and value in the home. In the black family, for instance, we are losing our sons and daughters not because of the weak moral values in our education system as well as the rest of society, we are losing them because of absenteeism. Fathers are not available; they are nowhere to be seen, and even those that are available, I am appalled at the lack of good moral support that is present in the home. The black family has become an "endangered species."

Os Hillman states,

> We live today when there is unprecedented breakdown in the family structure. Broken homes are major contributors to drug use, illegal sexual activity, and inability to secure gainful employment, jail sentences, and many other problems facing society today. For so many the choice that is being made is bringing the curse of God upon their lives and on the lives of their children and children's children…..The breaking of covenant in marriage is the source of the breakdown in the family today. This breakdown is the source of the bad fruit we are now experiencing worldwide, namely the four As, as Craig Hill of Family Foundations cites: adultery, addictions, abuse and abandonment. This fruit has further manifested into epidemic rates of divorce, gender confusion (gay and lesbian growth) and same-sex marriage.
>
> As a single parent and doing this for fifteen years, I have a story to tell. I have three children from my marriage. My husband abandoned us, left home when they were all in the middle of high school. I had two godly ladies in my life that represented my support system, Val and Vie—one is Vallretta and the other Valerie—and more importantly I had a big god. My daughter walked into my bedroom one afternoon and asked boldly, as if she was making an announcement, "Can my friend come to live with us?" I was shocked by her question, but did not give it a second thought or any

consideration because of the impossibility of that ever happening. So I responded, "What? Of course not." As usual, I thought she would back off and not push the subject any further because she, more than anyone else around me, knew and understood that I could never afford in our wildest imagination to do such a thing. My daughter has always been a "perfect" child, a type A personality, very mild mannered, rarely complains about anything, and is always extremely understanding, and most of all, is never aggressive or even assertive.

But I was surprised when she asked again in a rather serious tone, indicating that she was not joking but very serious about the question and wanted yes for an answer. So she proceeded to give an elaborate explanation why her friend must move in with us. The conversation went like this: "My friend was living with a lady in Hackensack. The lady was a friend of her parents, and the lady said that she cannot return to the house."

I asked inquisitively, "So where are her parents?"

"Her mother lives in Jamaica, and her father lives in Georgia."

"Why is she not living with her father?"

Questions continued from me, and the answers provided more reasons why it should be done. I cannot recall what convinced me to say yes or how I changed my mind. Needless to say, that young lady came to live with us and became the first of a list of ladies who came after, some temporarily, some adopted. Today, I am noted for my large family and large weddings in my home. Within five years, there were five weddings in my home because of one Christ-like decision. Today, this young lady is a wife, mother, educated professional, and an ardent worker in ministry who also functions as one of the praise team leaders. She was the first in a list of people who came into my life that has served to bring maturity spiritually, emotionally, and psychologically. That decision to say yes to help someone at seemingly the worst time in my life opened the flood gates of heaven into my heart, which aided my healing from the inside out. It was the ability to love others without conditions attached that helped me to see myself and understand that I was innately selfish and could not see that self-focus was equally as destructive as having someone abusing me from the outside. Yes, I was selfish and had no clue that I was, particularly since I was focused on the pain I was feeling from living for years in a very unhappy marriage. I was quietly mad at God for permitting me to experience unfairness in every capacity. I gave *my* love to people and received hate. I gave *my* money that I worked very hard to receive and in return received insults. I gave *my* stuff away and what do I get. I gave *my* heart away and ended up with nothing but pain. My reputation, I thought, was gone. Life was just plain unfair to me in every way, or so I thought.

I married for love, not looks. There is an inside joke in my family attached to this statement. I was only eighteen years old when it happened, but to date, I have never blamed anyone for the decision I made. I knew exactly what I was doing. So when I received the rude awakening only two months after my elaborate wedding, I knew immediately that I was in for a long, rough ride that only God himself could release me from. How easy it is for us to make choices that will impact our lives indefinitely, and how hard it is to reverse or correct those decisions. I never believed in divorce and by nature was always totally committed to any decision I made, so I was in this thing for the long haul. I knew that one day it would end, but I had no clue how it would happen or who would make it happen. I was dedicated and committed to my family and would do anything to make it work. So back to the question "can my friend move in" sent an array of emotion coursing through my veins. First of all, I was now a single mother with three children that I was unable to provide for adequately. Many days, they would walk to school with no lunch, walk back home, and ate whatever was available for a late lunch. They never complained despite the obvious pain and embarrassment I knew they were experiencing. In addition, our home was newly purchased, less than two years old. I also had my first car and the long list of expenses that came along with owning a home and a new car. I worked two jobs to make ends meet and still the ends were not being met. I was thoroughly involved in my church, completely miserable with the people I worshipped with more than five times per week. In retrospect, my only consolation was the devoted prayer life and life of worship I developed. I had absolutely no social life, and my friends amounted to two ladies as mentioned previously. How can God expect me to give out of nothing? I had no money to offer, very little food in the house, and barely enough to make a good meal on Sunday. I could not afford to buy clothes for my children; I could not afford to send them to school as I should. I could not afford to give them any direction in life. My life was in shamble, and I described myself as a woman with issues. It was at this point in my life when I was empty, feeling abandoned by a man who I gave everything I owned. My dignity was gone; I was embarrassed, frustrated, overwhelmed, and ashamed. But here I was at this moment in time, and God said I still have something to offer; I have my heart left, God's heart. Unknowingly, my heart was broken, but the easiest way to mend a broken heart was to love again. The road to my healing was in pouring out the love of Jesus Christ into others who needed to know that someone really cares. I dedicated myself from then on to develop excellent godly standard in my home. The path to my recovery was not in waiting for someone to come and love me. Rather, my recovery was grounded in my ability to receive the love of Jesus, open my heart in order for him to pour himself into it, thereby giving me the capacity to give something far more valuable than money or possession. I was giving like Christ did; I was giving away my heart in order for someone to have joy. All I had to offer was the strength of God that was growing in me. Wrapped by the power to love that was flowing in my heart is what I have become today, a role model, an example, a person with great spiritual values, a woman accomplished, a servant leader, a teacher, and much more. The birth of the new Joan began when I made a decision to open my home despite the pain and challenges I was experiencing and share things far more valuable than those offered by the world. Today, I am thanked so frequently for being an example. "You taught me how to pray. You taught me how to live. You taught me how to love, and you taught me how to share." Every day, I see Christians around me who like their personal space so much that it's reserved for their immediate family only. Their house is kept clean and locked away beautifully decorated with no feet to smudge the carpet or soil the furniture. Their stuff is protected with everything they have, the stuff that are temporary and carry no lasting value.

There is no sacrifice as powerful as giving away your life in order for someone to have life. In fact, real life begins when you give your life away so that someone else may live. I was reading the news today as I write of a four-year-old child who saw his three-year-old companion drowning in the swimming pool. The four-year-old boy unselfishly, without giving a second thought, dived into the bottom of the pool to save this child. He completely forgot that he was not able to swim. He did not think that he should go call for help like adults would do. All that he knew was that his friend was dying, and he knew that he must respond to save the life of his friend. He dived in and ended up losing his own life. That's God's nature. He wants us to dive in to help someone else without giving consideration to the results or whether or not it may benefit us in the long run. When it comes to giving ourselves away, the results are in the hands of God. Experience surely teaches wisdom. In my short life, I have come to realize that it is always better to give than to receive as Jesus Christ stated. For it is in giving that we find true fulfillment. I am amazed by the volume of Christians who I come across with that simply do not demonstrate the love of Christ in their daily walk. Most people I know are self-focused. They do not share their homes, their cars, their money, their time, their clothes, and their contacts with the people around them who are visibly in need. Even in church, I see people care about their personal ministries, education, etc., rather than the collective success of the people they encounter every day. Many are far removed from the lives of the people they rub shoulders with frequently. They go to work and church and return home to invest in their affairs without giving consideration to the needs of the people around them.

Christ as the Example

On observing the life of Jesus Christ as I read the Bible, it is so evident that Jesus was always focused on the needs of the people he encountered. He was deliberate in his service to his community. He went looking for people he could impact every day. He fed them before teaching them about God. He healed them. He healed their family members. He prayed for them. He taught them how to live and love God first. Jesus lived completely for others, and he was strategic about it. Every move he made was to benefit the poor, the sick, the reject, the lost, and dying. He was in the business of empowering people. We talk about Jesus every day; we sing about him, we preach about him, we teach about him, yet we struggle to become like him. It is almost like we have him right in front of us but cannot become like him. Oh, how far away he is from our hearts. We teach about the love of Christ but have great difficulty living what we preach. The greatest challenge for any individual is to honor the words we speak. It is easy to tell everyone else what to do with their lives, but the challenge is always, "Can I practice what I preach? Can I live the things I expect from everyone else?" Jesus was never focused on his own needs. In fact, he created very few problems for himself by living simple. Life gets complicated when we own too much, want too much, expect too much, and do too much. Many of us stretch ourselves too thin to prove to others that we are accomplished. The world is filled with extremists; some of us are overachievers, while others are underachievers. Everyone can maintain a relatively balanced life by living a life that is more purpose driven. Understanding my purpose gave me focus and provided me with the will to plan for extras. Everything I do apart from what I was born to do is merely extras.

Jesus life was uncluttered with stuff and people. He had three people in his inner circle and twelve disciples who he chose to follow him around until his assignment was completed. The rest of the people were free to enter his life briefly and leave. Most of them were encountered in his quest to preach the kingdom of God. Jesus was focused, strategic, and unencumbered by stuff. He chose not to own a house, he chose not to be committed to a personal family, and he chose to simplify his life in order to make time for ministry. His ministry was his assignment on earth. He had friends, as in Lazarus, Mary, and Martha. But the amazing thing was that he loved the world. When Jesus touched the life of one person, it was equal to touching thousands because the transformation that would take place in that person propelled the person to share the experience with others. Just like the woman at the well. She was not condemned and judged by Christ, rather she was healed from her issues. The weaknesses that she struggled with for many years made her ashamed. She was rejected by an entire community, particularly those who saw her as a threat to their love life and family. But Jesus forgave her of her sins, delivered her from weaknesses, brought restoration to her life, and gave her a brand new start. You see, with God, there is absolutely nothing that is impossible; we can all start over. What a wonderful thing to begin again. You may have failed in the past, but with Christ, we can make the decision to start again. There is never any failure in God.

I could have chosen to give up when my world was torn apart by a broken marriage. In fact, on some days, I thought that I was on the verge of losing my mind. But my recovery began when I opened my home and my heart to others. My home became the meeting place for teenagers from the church. They would come for dinner after church on Sunday. For years, my dining room chair carried a large stain on the cushion's cloth because someone spilled a jug of famous red juice on the chair. I recall one night I went to bed tired after an exhausting day. I had a dream that cars were packed into my driveway with one car protruding into the street. I woke up with a startle, went to check, and sure enough, there was a large, old beaten up car sticking out of my driveway. I knocked on one of the room doors and heard something like a million feet scurrying into the attic. They were running for dear life because it was two in the morning. Today, many of those same kids are leaders in their churches, including pastors. The most interesting story concerns my daughter's husband, the current youth pastor of our church. He was the friend of my son. We did not like him. We thought he was bad influence, straight from the street of Paterson. Every time we cooked and left the dinner on the stove for everyone to help themselves, my son would show up with this kid. They would eat without giving consideration to anyone else, then disappear. Their thing was basketball. I remember though, one day I took that kid, sat him down at the foot of my bed where all my counseling sessions took place, and encouraged him to do right. I am not sure whether that had any impact on his life, but with the help of God and his seriously praying mother, God saved him from the street. He is our church's youth pastor today. Hallelujah! God can change anyone. His son Isaiah is my first grandchild from my three birth children. The ministry that began in my home was made possible by the godly standards I set.

Standard in the Church

After our church was built, dinner was no longer held in my house but at the church every Sunday at 3 p.m. Every Sunday, I cooked the rice and bean all ten pounds of it and served in the kitchen. On many days, there was not enough for everyone, but we found a way to make it work. The crowd simply grew from twenty-five to accommodate all ages. I found more fulfillment in serving others. It was a beauty to wash the concrete basement floor, clean the kitchen, serve meals with a smile, decorate the church, do the gardens, and more. When people are happy, I became happy. Something great was happening to me on the inside. Transformation was taking place because I was demonstrating Christ-like attributes. I developed a holy discontent for those who were not treated right. I supported godly decisions, Christ-like behavior, justice, peace, the fruits of the spirit, and hated lies and injustice. I was either loved or hated, and without titles or positions, I became a leader in my own right. My gift was making room for me. I was like a butterfly in its period of transformation. I was born shy, grew up shy, did not speak in college, reserved, and as a result, many misunderstood me and described me as proud. But it was increasingly becoming evident that the hands of God were on my life. Everything I saw that I knew God hated, I hated. Everything that opposed God's nature, I would not support. I was rejected from the cliques, treated sometimes with disdain, preached upon from the pulpit, ridiculed, and embarrassed but would somehow rise above it. I would ignore the annoyances around me, pray for the church to become like Christ, interceded for the pastor, and stood my ground for everything I knew was right. I was developing a lonely life. I could see people look at me with respect and amazement but did not dare to publicly support me because of how they may be treated. Only the brave gave me support publicly, and by association, my two friends testify today of some of the experiences they had because they took the risk of being my friend.

I was lonely for the company of people but was hungry to know more about God. My extra time was spent in prayer and worship. I would sometimes go home crying from words that people spoke that meant me harm but would return to the next service with worship. I never stopped going to church. I never argued with anyone. I never chose to get mad with God. I never compromised but trusted God to deliver me from this season in my life. Something amazing was happening all at the same time. At home, I was getting accustomed to living as a father and mother to my children. At church, I was finding my place in the center of a circle of people who built alliances and publicly showed that they were against me. I still smiled with them, loved them, respected them, supported them in ministry, and encouraged them publicly. I decided that I would die for the things of God and would stand for the things that Jesus stood for, even if I became friendless. God sent many people into my life during my lonely period to bring words of encouragement that would serve to keep me moving forward. Amazingly, I never gave thought of leaving my church, never gave thought of becoming a pastor, and never gave thought to relocate to another state. I trusted God to take care of me despite the challenges. Pain is pain, and I felt great emotional pain—some brought about by the rejection I felt from home and church, other types of pain from being disappointed by the quality of the lifestyle I saw some Christians led. I saw people hurt each other's feelings without any consideration. Those made me pray even more for transformation in my life as well as the church. I saw jealousy, envy, and strife from some, but there were others who I respected for their love, faithfulness, generosity of spirit, and Christ-like attributes, and I gravitated automatically to them. I knew I was different from most people around, and on reflection today, I can now see that God was preparing me for my future and purpose. I was simply in training. The tears, the pain, the grief, the rejection, and the discomfort were all birthing out a level of maturity in me that would be critical in the future for building a church. When the predestined time comes, God will make it happen, and it will be unstoppable. In Matthew chapter one, at the birth of Jesus, his ancestry was clearly documented and established as it relates to David and Abraham. The Jews, more than any other culture of the day, understood what it meant to be related to Abraham and David, and they looked forward to the coming of the Messiah as declared by the prophets. The issue is they were not expecting a Messiah with humble beginnings. The meaning of the name Jesus is God with us. It was time for the Messiah to be revealed to mankind, and it was done at the right time—fourteen generations from Abraham to David and fourteen generations from David to the birth of the Messiah. God's timing is always right. Only God knows when and how to offer us to the world. He will not do it prematurely neither will he do it according to man's personal desires. We sometimes get more than we can bear, but a way of escape is always made so that we are able to bear it. Suddenly, my personal and spiritual life began to change right in front of my eyes. I was appointed to teach a small Sunday school class. My name was gaining popularity among the small mass of people in sister churches.

Simultaneously, I was promoted on my job to become the executive director. This experience still amazes me every time I think about the power of God's grace. I took a low paid job at Irvington Public Library and decided that I would stay for one year because I did not like the location, the town, or the distance from where I lived. After a couple months on the job, I was asked to become the head of the children's department because the person who headed the department left. That position brought visibility to the library because new methods of programming were introduced. I restructured the entire department, streamlined processes, and marketed new children's services. My name was everywhere in town. All this was done without a salary increase. I did not think of asking for an increase. This was the stepping-stone to my professional career as a library director. After approximately four years, I became discontented because I felt that it was time for a promotion of some sort. I was shocked when an emergency meeting was called by the library director, and she announced her retirement. Not only was she retiring but the assistant director was also retiring early. I knew that God was up to something. So I decided that I would pursue one of the positions. I applied for the position of assistant director. Other employees applied as well for the position of director and assistant director. To my amazement, a director was hired, and I was informed that the director would make his decision when to hire an assistant.

The new director destroyed years of hard work that was put in place to build the institution, and the majority of the staff left, including me. I was confused by what God was doing but trusted him as he was developing his character in me. I became the director of a small public library five minutes from my home. The job was boring with the absence of challenge and fulfillment. I showed up for work to get a paycheck and oftentimes wondered where my life headed. One night at 11 p.m., I received the call that changed my life forever. The board president for the Irvington Public Library was on the phone. An offer was made to me to return to my job as the director of the library. My promotion at work paralleled my promotion at church. God was raising me up in both places at the same time. It was incredible; things were falling in place, and it was done without any effort on my part. It was favor at work, and as they say, "favor is not fair."

Establishing a Firm Foundation

Nowhere in the Scriptures have I seen where God chose leaders who were ill-prepared or untrained. There is generally a firm foundation that is built from hard work, life experiences, trials, conflicts, suffering, etc. God's work necessitates faithfulness in order for completion to take place. His ways are different from that of humans. That's why he chose an impossible journey for the Israelites to follow going to that place of promise. The journey was divided into phases, and every stop was strategically designed for them to get to know him better. While they built their relationship with him, invaluable life lessons would be learned along the way. If they had proven themselves, they would become solid examples to the surrounding cultures and nations and become the blueprint of how Jehovah would be introduced to other cultures. Israel was chosen to represent God to the world. Their responses to the challenges were disappointing, yet despite that fact, God kept his unconditional covenants with them and continued to exercise his mercy. While by his nature, God exercised justice and could not ignore sin; on the other hand, by his nature he showed mercy and compassion.

The Hebrews began the journey right but failed to continue in the same mindset by disrespecting God and the leader he chose. They disrespected God because he did not work according to their schedules and needs. For instance, God gave them manna, but they wanted meat and the provisions they were accustomed to in Egypt. They consistently reminded Moses of the past and how good they had it going for them. They thought that if only they could just get back the food they had, then everything would be better. How unappreciative we sometimes become when we do not have it our way. We must learn to build a solid foundation by doing the following:

- Give thanks for everything, even the small things.

- Sacrifice for the greater good. Give something for a greater cause.
- Remain humble and obedient at every phase of the journey.
- Remain broken before God; seek him, pray without ceasing, and trust his word.
- Remain faithful. Never stop. Keep putting one foot before the other.
- Think positively; always think the best of everything, including people.
- Maintain a teachable spirit; you do not know it all.

Just like any good building under construction, the foundation is vital to the integrity of the building. During times of inclement weather, earthquakes, war, and everyday wear and tear, the building must be able to withstand the test of time. Our lives are no exception because for sure, whether we desire to or not, we cannot prevent problems. They come in all kinds of packages. God himself sometimes changes the rules on us. As he relates to Israel, one day he will tell you to strike the rock, and another day he will tell you to speak to the rock. It is entirely up to him to move in a different direction. We must be prepared to follow as he leads. Remember, there is always a reason for the "madness" when it comes to God, and it is always meant to bring us closer to him.

Bless Me Indeed and Enlarge My Territories

A new believer was missing from church for several months. I approached her as she stopped by one day, took her into my office, and like any good pastor, inquired how she was faring. The response shocked me somewhat, she said, "This church thing is not working for me because everything I was expecting did not happen." It amazes me when people who, I believe should know better, act inappropriately. They go to God with a laundry list of requests. Once they do not receive the items on the list, they become depressed, discouraged, and disappointed. This is generally exhibited in their behavior pattern, which spills over into their interaction with people. God's blessings are packaged differently from the devil's blessings. The world blesses you first and then you pay the price later. God proves you first and then he blesses you later. Along the journey, God gave strict commandments for his people to follow. There were ten major ones and hundreds of smaller ones in the form of ordinances and statutes. The law was the law; if it was broken, there were consequences. Thank God for grace that came with a better covenant. In Deuteronomy 28, blessings were promised to the entire Hebrew nation. They were blessed in the city and in the field, in their going out and in their coming in. They were the head and not the tail. Most people read without realizing that these were conditional blessings. The condition is if you keep his statutes and commandments, these blessings would follow. If not, the following curses would follow you.

Kingdom Blessings

It is important to note that God desires to bless everyone. However, we have a responsibility to practice and live by the Word of God. The kingdom of God has a completely different set of rules than the kingdom of the world. The blessing plan of God is better explained from a kingdom perspective. The kingdom of God is the rule of an eternal sovereign God over all creatures and things. The kingdom of God is also the designation for the sphere of salvation entered into at the new birth and is synonymous with the kingdom of heaven. Anyone who accepts God's leadership and is subject to him is a part of the kingdom. Born again believers become a part of the kingdom of God. The kingdom of God and the kingdom of heaven are one and the same and cannot be separated in definition. The kingdom of the world is dominated by Satan, the god of the world. The kingdom of the world is visible. It appears real and right. It says put yourself first. The kingdom of the world says that you are more important than anyone around you. Think about yourself first and everyone after. Do it your way because your interests matter more. Your god is here to help you succeed, and he will understand. The kingdom of the world says go with the majority, fit in, and religion and God are not really necessary. Gamble, negotiate, cheat, and do what you have to do to get to the top. Be tough, mean, and aggressive; just be first. Seek power, fame, money, and recognition for that's the way to be happy. Especially if your parents were not very successful, go for it and prove to everyone that you can make it; do better than they did. It says truth is relative, and you have a right to your opinion.

We are either a part of the kingdom of God or the kingdom of the world. The kingdom of God says sex is reserved for your spouse of the opposite sex. Practice self-control, and do not live for immediate gratification. The kingdom of God says be content, love everyone, including your enemies. The kingdom of God says do not worry about what you shall eat or drink or about life. Life is more than food and raiment. The kingdom of God says we are lost without a savior and will end up in hell. Blessed are the meek. Blessed are the peacemakers. Blessed are the pure in heart. Blessed are the merciful. The kingdom of God says thou shall not and nothing is impossible with God. The kingdom of God says love, joy, peace, long-suffering, gentleness, meekness, and self-control is the law. Two separate value systems face us every day, and we must know the distinctions. The kingdom is at the heart of God's plan for humanity from the outset and throughout history. It began in Genesis, and according to Revelation, it will conclude time as we know it. The destiny of every human being, every race, nation, ethnic group, and tribe is inextricably tied to God's kingdom plan or order. God's eternal plan for humanity began when he designed a perfect place for man called the Garden of Eden. Satan is well aware of God's kingdom order and intervened and disrupted the plan temporarily. Thereafter, God began to deal with the Israelites at the call of Abraham. God's goal was to bring back the kingdom plan on Earth, which he started in Eden. So he called Abraham and made non -conditional promises to him. God chose a race who would adopt his kingdom plan on Earth, and as he blessed them, they would transfer or spread his kingdom to the four corners of the Earth. God began to deal with Israel by developing a theocratic form of government, which was always with a judge, king, or prophet who heard from God and led the people or nation depending on God's desire. There was a common threat in every covenant made. At the core of each was the kingdom order. Notice that every time the children of Israel obeyed God, they were blessed, and when they disobeyed, they were cursed. The kingdom order is based upon strict obedience to God's word. It will not work any other way. Failure and frustration will result when men's plan are introduced. God's kingdoms presence changes atmosphere and situations, and wherever and whenever there is rebellion, disobedience, sin, and anything contrary to the kingdom principles, there is no favor from God. "Seek ye first the kingdom of God and His righteousness and all these things shall be added" Matthew 6:33 (kjv).

Power Points of This Chapter

- History has proven that God has chosen those of us with very little influence, money, social standing, and political power and use us to change the world.
- The world blesses you first and then you pay the price later. God proves you first and then he blesses you later.

- We are either a part of the kingdom of God or the kingdom of the world.
- The destiny of every human being, every race, nation, ethnic group, and tribe is inextricably tied to God's kingdom plan or order.

Managing Success

> This book of the law shall not depart from your mouth but you shall meditate upon it day and night, that you may observe to do all that is written in it. For then you shall make your way prosperous, and then you shall have good success.
>
> Joshua 1:8 (KJV)

What Is Success?

The word "success" has a variety of definitions depending on your perspective. The popular definition of success is compatible with the accumulation of material things such as money, power, fame, honor, level of education, etc. Words such as accomplishment and attainment are used to describe success as they relate to goals, purpose, and outcome, as well as the former material things previously itemized. Popular definitions are all directly related to individual personal accomplishment. While that is partially true, for me, it's a little more than my personal accomplishment that defines me as successful. Success is attaining your goals, living in your place of promise, spiritual maturity, changing your sphere of influence, and leaving a legacy behind you that will impact lives, even after you're gone. I have always asked my children to put a simple epithet on my headstone at burial, which goes like this: "The woman who obeyed

God first, then man after." This describes who I am and should describe the substance and nature of the life we lead. For in our obedience to God, we are also able to submit and obey superiors, as well as those who have interest in our lives. Anyone who desires to be successful must first become humble and learn to submit to the small and the great. I have seen so many young men and women who are so anxious to be successful that they become driven by pride and an overzealous passion to get to the top. Getting to our place of promise prematurely can become self-destructive. Lack of experience and training that can only be gathered by years of learning life lessons can be a detriment rather than a benefit. It is of vital importance that we understand that God works with the time we live in from eternity. The stops along the way teach great lessons that we are able to utilize later. In fact, timing is a law all by itself. If we disrupt the timing of God for our lives by consistently taking matters into our hands, then we will for sure suffer the consequences of our immature behavior. Remember, there is a price for success, and there is a cost for even the call of God upon our lives. Real success should not be attained overnight. The majority of teenage stars, for example in the secular, oftentimes struggle with a host of internal psychological issues because of premature fame and stardom. Their friends are generally shallow and hypocritical because they are present due to the possibility that they may benefit from the relationship. They oftentimes lack the ability to manage stress, crisis, and money and sometimes seek life-destructive solutions to deal with the pain of their circumstances. They correspondingly have stuff, power, and money but live without peace, real joy, and fulfillment. The ability to wait is an invaluable tool. Skills are not developed overnight. Waiting until a good level of personal confidence and security is developed is crucial to longevity. Joshua, for instance, submitted to Moses as his leader, mentor, and coach and worked side by side with Moses who had a far greater level of experience. Along with the experience, he garnered his own personality trait; Israel gave birth to another mighty world changer. Joshua was chosen at the right time for the job. The law of timing was applied to his life when God announced, "Arise. Go over this Jordan, you and all this people." Joshua was not aware that it was the right time. Only God knows when we are ready, and he will speak at the exact moment directly or indirectly. Notice Joshua waited for forty long years at the feet of Moses. He did not usurp authority or seek to underhandedly betray Moses as Absalom did to his father, David. Joshua was not in the limelight; scriptures did not mention him much, only on occasions when it was needful to document his response as he gave support to Moses. According to John Maxwell, "It took 40 years for Joshua's leadership style to match the need of the moment." His character and personality were molded and tweaked by God for forty years to prepare him for years of combat that awaited him. He continued as Moses did by consulting God first prior to making a decision. He remained humble, took the lead in warfare, and always gave the credit to God. Some leaders are called to initiate and develop a project, while others are called to implement and conclude a project. Moses was the initiator and developer, while Joshua was the implementer. A completely new set of skills were needed to possess the land. Joshua's skills were appropriate for this new season in Israel's lives.

- Success is maintaining a spirit of excellence, even when the resources are minimal.
- Success is thinking right during times of crisis, even when the enemy launches his attacks against your life.
- Success is stability. It is making a resolve that you will not be moved from where you are placed by God.
- Success is speaking right and making the right decisions at the right place and at the right time.
- Success is maintaining character and integrity in your place of promise.
- Success is remaining humble after fame, honor, and accomplishment.
- Success is living your life on purpose.

Success is not:

- Placing material things above values, principle, and character.
- Wandering around in circles.
- Disrespecting people because of your accomplishments.
- Living proud and allowing greed to become your driving force.

Managing Success

The children of Israel entered the promise land, and immediately, they were presented with a whole new set of challenges. As I mentioned earlier, it is important that we take time to celebrate our accomplishments. It is said that greater levels bring greater devils. Success comes with its own set of challenges, so before we begin to deal with the new problems, we must celebrate. Stop or pause and take a time out with friends, family, and colleagues to laugh, have fun, fellowship, and thank God and everyone who made the journey possible. There is a brilliant strategy for managing success that is outlined in Joshua chapter 8:1–29. Joshua and his soldiers made a grave mistake by miscalculating their ability to defeat the city of Ai. They did not properly consult God for guidance but became a little too arrogant and compromised. Achan secretly stole some of the spoils of war and dishonored the command of God. They were specifically told not to take anything from the spoils of war. They quickly learned from their mistake and changed their attitude. The strategy is God should be consulted for directives. The directives were used as a foundation for planning. I am noted to be both spiritual and practical. There is a saying that I use frequently in my church that goes like this: "After I get down or up from being high in the spirit, I have some good common sense." Joshua knew how to plan effectively after consultation with God.

John Maxwell asked the question, "When does faith become presumption, expecting God to do for us what we must grab hold of ourselves?" Every human being must have a plan in place for their lives. We cannot live haphazardly and expect to achieve or maintain success. There must be a balance between faith and planning. It is in preparation that we are able to weather the difficult times and solve the problems as they arise. God gave the general direction, and Joshua filled in the details of the battle strategy. When God says move and you are unsure what to do, develop a plan by seeking the directives of the Holy Spirit. Always measure your plan against the Word of God. If it's consistent with the Word, then proceed; if it's compromising, then don't follow through. While we were in the process of purchasing our very first church building, the Giant, we knew without any doubt that it was pointed out by God. That fact kept us focused. With much prayer, we proceeded to hire a realtor, an attorney, architect, accountant, and a mortgage broker. We worked tirelessly with these professionals to develop strategic plans, business plans, architectural plans, and budgets, as well as the necessary legal paperwork to support the purchase. After submitting applications to over twenty banks and denied by all twenty, we never gave up. Finally, during prayer and much thought, I was given a boost of confidence by the Holy Spirit, and I knew that one of the three final offers on the table would work. I called the mortgage broker, selected one of the offers, and within weeks, we closed on the property. We utilized our training, experience, common sense, and resources, and through sheer hard work, we accomplished the impossible.

Managing success involves knowing the following:

- Never operate through ego because pride destroys your integrity. It takes a lifetime to establish integrity and one mistake to destroy it.
- It is never about you. It is always about others. Seek to empower people when you have accomplished your dreams. Help others to succeed by investing your time, energy, and resources into them.
- You cannot solve world hunger by yourself, but you can make a difference from where you are. Seek to become a world changer by positively encouraging people within your sphere of influence.
- Surround yourself with the right people. Your inner circle must consist of those people who will watch your back. These people you can count on even when you fail or fall.
- Build relationships with everyone including those with the characteristics of Rahab. She was not a Hebrew, neither powerful nor influential but she was street smart and recognized that her future depended on the help she offered.
- Never take people for granted because you never know when you may need to call upon them.
- Communicate effectively, particularly to the team you lead and to the people you have delegated tasks and responsibilities.

- Maintain a teachable spirit by always listening, reading, and learning until you die. You will never know everything.
- Be strong and work consistently and smart.

Look at Me Now. I Have Made It

As I was writing the last chapters of this book, I moved my desk to my bedroom window during hurricane Sandy. The electricity in the house went out, which is where I set up my temporary office space. I pulled back the curtains as I directly faced the window to watch the storm. It was autumn, and the leaves acted as if they are whipped from the trees by an invisible hand. Huge dark clouds were rolling across the entire span of the atmosphere, and I saw the goodness of God in all the chaos. Storms are characterized by boisterous winds and rain. They are sometimes accompanied with an eye, like this hurricane. Every storm passes, and even during the middle of the storm, there is a short break from the turbulence as the eye passes over. During this time, you are able to regroup and re-strengthen yourself for the next half. God is comparable to the eye of the storm. He reaches in and creates a sense of peace and security, even during the most difficult times. Storms are necessary, the wind is valuable, and the rain is needed. It's all about your perspective. Seasons come and seasons go, and life continues. I should have been a statistic living like the beautiful, attractive young ladies I grew up with who matured and seemingly have not moved from Egypt. On my frequent visits to the place where I was born, in that small village, I saw those beautiful faces smiling with age and the stress and trauma that their journey has created. They have gathered years of experience but have not accomplished much. They continue in large part to struggle as their parents did and as their children and grandchildren will.

So I ask the question, "What exactly have I done to be looking through my bedroom window, through those leaves blowing violently through the wind, yet protected from the elements in a large house overlooking the Hudson River?" By some standards, I have arrived at my place of promise, but looking back, I can conclude that it's not the destination that matters. For me, the real deal is the journey. The significance of my life lies in the experiences along the way. So to answer the question, I cannot give credit to myself, particularly when I reflect on the stops along the way and the intensity of some of the painful experiences. It was the hand of God on my life, protecting me, keeping me, guiding me, sustaining me, strengthening me, teaching me, and delivering me that has collectively brought me to my destination. "Look at me now" means look at God; how capable he is of taking one life and directing that life from start to finish. Of course, my personality, internal drive to achieve, commitment, and dedication assisted to some degree, but those characteristics only helped but could not have made me into who I am today. Against all odds, I have made it to where I am today because of God's grace and mercy. I remember living in my first rented house in America and was told by my landlord that I would never have what she had. Unable to pay my rent on time and as I should, I was humiliated and embarrassed because of circumstances beyond my control. Today, those days are far gone and have not left me bitter and resentful but have contributed to my maturity and experience. Financial problems, like any other challenge, are part of the journey, and with God's help and good planning, it will be resolved.

I see the fruits of my labor today, and I'm able to enjoy weddings, grandchildren, church, friends, and an extended family while I serve God with all my heart. I am determined to teach, mentor, encourage, and share the small and large things I have accumulated with as many people as possible. I am in the promise land and look to a future where I seek to impact lives for the better. My giants are huge, but I see them as bread just as how Joshua saw them when they spied out the land. I intend to move from glory to glory. As I wrote, I looked down on my phone, and there was a text message from one of the leaders in my church. I was sent the telephone number of a pastor in Texas who I have not spoken with for many months. I was compelled to give him a call. He picked up on the first ring and was shocked because he was literally looking at my number to give me a call. He was excited to hear my voice and quickly explained that he was in the middle of one of the greatest storms in his life. I could hear the stress and pressure in his voice as the circumstances were attempting to rob him of his joy. He sounded aged even though he is quite young. His young daughter was battling with a brain tumor and was wheelchair bound. There were several major challenges happening all at the same time in his ministry. Plans were not being materialized for the new church. Significant people were leaving the church during great financial constraints. Finally, on his way from church, he was arrested for not carrying his driver's license, and his daughter eventually died. I listened attentively with empathy and then responded concerned. I shared the title of the book I was writing and explained to him the book's premise. The encouragement I gave him consisted of the following:

In the midst of our quagmires and afflictions God will give us peace. We must also have a balance between faith and planning in the midst of our turmoil. While we pray, we must work our plan, tweak our plan, go back to the drawing board, but never give up. Sooner or later, something will give.

Power Points of This Chapter

- Success, is attaining your goals, living in your place of promise, spiritual maturity, changing your sphere of influence, and leaving a legacy behind that will impact lives, even after you are gone.
- When God says move and you are unsure what to do, develop a plan by seeking the directives of the Holy Spirit.
- Every storm passes, and even during the middle of the storm, there is a short break from the turbulence as the eye passes over.

Dealing with the Enemy

> But I say unto you, Love your enemies, bless them that curse you, do good to them that hate you, and pray for them which despitefully use you, and persecute you.
>
> Matthew 5:44 (KJV)

When you are transitioned into your place of promise, you will be sleeping with the enemy. What do I mean? You will be living on their property, the property that was really meant for you. Expect trouble from the enemy when God blesses you. Remember Satan is consistent; he has no new tricks. He is not creative, period. God beats him every time because God is creative and because he knows how to change his strategies by creating new ones; every battle is the Lord's. It is paramount today that you do not see your enemies as people but as the devil, the deceiver, Satan, the father of lies. It is the spirit of Satan that is the driving force and the motivator behind every scheme to sabotage your destiny. His desire is to send you back into slavery, or even around the mountain. He wants to steal your inheritance, rob you of your joy, and keep you in a place of subservience. You can never negotiate with Satan. Remember it began all the way back in the Garden of Eden when he attempted to thwart God's plan for humanity. His desire is always to keep you enslaved to your situation and circumstances. He does not want you to keep moving from one phase of the journey to another. He wants you to remain in the wilderness, not for forty years but rather for your entire life, grumbling and complaining, never taking responsibility for your actions or behavior. Satan's desire is to keep you thinking small with low expectations. He loves when you wake up in misery, live in dysfunctional family environment, barely surviving.

On the contrary, God has a plan for your life; He loves you and thinks good thoughts about you. You were designed by God to become successful and achieve greatness. God specializes in taking people from obscurity to a place of prominence. God has the best for all of us without any exception. He will take any individual irrespective of our background, ethnicity, culture, etc., and deliver us from self-destructive behaviors, molestation, insecurities, drug addictions, and violent tendencies and release us into living on purpose. I would not exchange my life with Christ for any other lifestyle. I love who I am and desire to share my personal relationship with God to the world. Jesus came with the greatest mission ever introduced to mankind. I have had the opportunity to study comparative religion recently, and after analyzing their foundational teachings and principles, I realized that Christianity is the only religion with a loving savior who died to redeem us from our sins. He liberated us completely on the cross, rose from the dead on the third day, and returned to the right hand of God, with only one condition; we must believe by faith. We are offered a personal relationship with God without works. It is a free gift from God, and by grace, we are saved. Being born again represents a new life where we are sanctified and regenerated through Christ's death and resurrection. We are given what's called abundant life. Jesus declares, "Seek ye first the kingdom of God and his righteousness and all these things shall be added unto you" Matthew 6:33 (KJV). The exception is that we must take up our cross and follow him. In other words, we must participate in his sufferings. The art of war must be employed in order to dispossess the enemy. Engaging the enemy must be done with precision, wisdom, and at the right time. Some enemies appear to be friends, while others are proactive in proving to you that they are your enemies. Whatever face they present, enemies are dangerous, yet we are encouraged by Christ to love our enemies, bless those who curse us, and pray for those who despitefully use us. We can learn a few lessons from the children of Israel as they engage the enemy in order to dispossess them. Remember through Christ, the weapon of our warfare is not carnal but mighty with the pulling down of strongholds, casting down imaginations and every high thing that exalts itself against the knowledge of God. We, however, can learn invaluable strategies from the actions of Israel toward the enemy as they move to possess the land. Let's examine briefly some of those employed:

- Joshua and his warriors failed at the first attempt when they came against the small city of Ai. They became overly confident because of their precious victory over Jericho and thought that this would be an easy victory for them. They failed miserably by miscalculating the strength of the enemy. God was not very supportive of their victory this time around because they broke the rule of integrity. We must maintain our integrity whether things are going well for us or not. For unknown reasons, one person offended God, and everyone paid the penalty. The problem was removed when it was discovered, they regained their rightful position with God, and they had a decisive victory. God will not bless us in our mess, but he will honor a life of truth and integrity. We must remove the wrong and make it right with him. We cannot compromise, even under pressure. The same standards we begin with, we must end the journey with. Character outweighs gifts any day and will keep us where God has placed us, in our place of promise.

- On entering the promise land, Joshua and the entire nation faced a new challenge. It was dealing with the enemies collectively. The surrounding tribes became united to fight against Israel because they heard about the defeat of Jericho. One tribe, the Gibeonites, pretended to be on the side of Israel but with the intent to sabotage Israel's destiny. They sent ambassadors to Israel dressed as if they were living in poverty, lied that they were from a far country, and wanted to become servants of Israel by making a covenant. Joshua and the rest of Israel made a covenant with these people without consulting

God. The truth was revealed in a matter of days that these people were imposters and were close neighbors and real enemies. Israel must honor its promise to these people and ultimately permitted them to live. Israel failed again to remove the enemy from the land because they compromised their spiritual values. One of the greatest weapons against the enemy is to maintain our values and principles. These are never worth compromising. As in this situation, the enemy is always afraid of the people of God; he is the one that is intimidated, not us. In the long run, Israel gained victory after victory because they learned from their mistake during this season. According to Joshua 11:23, "So Joshua took the whole land, according to all that the Lord said unto Moses; and Joshua gave it for an inheritance unto Israel according to their divisions by their tribes. And the land rested from war."

The Power of Prayer

We cannot and should not underestimate the power of prayer. One of the greatest weapons against the enemy is the ability to communicate with God through prayer. We are directed to pray without ceasing. This does not mean that we spend long hours praying every day. What it means is that we are constantly positioned mentally, spiritually, and emotionally to speak to God and to listen to his responses. Prayer is communication, it is essential that we seek, ask, and knock consistently until we see results. Of even more importance is listening. We must stop, wait, and listen. Oftentimes, we are told that we should only ask God once because he hears us the first time. There is scriptural evidence to prove that our prayers can be blocked by supernatural forces as was the case with the prayer of Daniel later in Israel's history. While God has the ability to do anything he wants to do, Satan is the reigning king of the kingdom of the world. Satan has, at his command, demons that by their nature are not omnipresent, but they are agents that are given assignments and directives. We must be careful that we pray against the agents of the enemy.

Prayer is giving God permission to act on earth on our behalf. According to Dr. Cindy Trimm, "It is in prayer that we probe spiritual realities, communicate with God, access the arsenal of heaven, and expand God's kingdom on the earth. It is as simple as pulling aside to a quiet place and opening your heart to God, and as dynamic as tapping into the power and imagination that created the cosmos." There are times when the answer is not in the affirmative for a number of reasons, sometimes unknown. However, it is essential that we maintain our confidence in the face of fear and continue to exercise our faith. Oftentimes, God does not grant our request because the timing is just not right or the request, if granted, may create more harm than good. We must, however, remain vigilant in prayer. For me, it is my faithfulness in prayer that brings great results. Every major crisis I have faced in ministry or my personal life has worked out in victory because I am relentless in prayer. The strategy is I gather my prayer support group and agree beforehand that we are bringing the matter to God to be resolved. We sometimes do not ask for a precise solution, but we pray according to the will of God for our lives. We do not stop until we see results or a conclusion to the crisis. Sometimes during the process, it is painful, especially when we are involved emotionally, but we always remain focused with full confidence that even if he does not deliver, he remains a faithful God.

Sometimes, we experience death instead of life. Sometimes, we lose the deal on the table, but the majority of times, we come out laughing after the pain and discomfort. Prayer destroys strongholds, break yokes, and remove spiritual systems that have been established by the enemy to stop us from living a fruitful life. Prayer brings us closer to God. It takes us into the presence of God, builds intimacy with God, and thereby minimizes the significance of the problems we encounter. The closer you are to God, the less impact the vicissitudes of life will have on your mind. You will never be consumed by grief, emotional, and psychological burdens when you remain faithful in prayer. The enemy's desire is to displace you and confuse your thinking by leading you to believe that the issues of life are of most importance. You can have problems but do not be overcome by them. We can raise ourselves above the issues of life and continue to think right, act right, and behave right. Do not compromise your values; honor your word and fight the enemy with integrity. Prayer keeps us grounded and removes the everyday stress from our minds that we struggle with as we search for answers to the variety of complex and simple problems we encounter. Like meditation, prayer relaxes the mind, unclutter our thoughts, and refocus us on what's important. It removes bitterness, envy, hate, grumbling, complaining, and the like and reminds us that we are loved by God and that we are significant and have purpose on our lives. The approval and affirmation we often seek from people will disappear with a disciplined prayer life. Let's find a quiet place with God every day, be alone in his presence where we connect in a genuine way, and ask for his guidance and direction in our everyday affairs. For if we pray without ceasing, decision making becomes easier. The right decisions bring the right results.

In the Scriptures, prayer provided answers and directions from God; it opened prison doors for Paul, Peter, and others and changed situations that are seemingly impossible to possible. Prayer works on an individual level as well on a broader scope. It changes families, communities, and nations. When the diagnosis from the doctors is negative, prayer changes things. Everyone in our church, since its inception, who has been diagnosed with major diseases, life threatening illnesses, and a multitude of "minor" health-related problems have seen the mighty hand of God heal and deliver them from sickness. We have yet to have a funeral. Our first and only funeral was that of the mother of my adopted daughter who refused to accept Christ as her lord and savior repeatedly.

I am compelled to share the story of my brother's healing from a massive aneurism. A few years ago, my brother moved into my home temporarily due to family issues. He is a diabetic, and we were aware that he was sick but felt that it was minor and did not address the situation aggressively. He refused to visit the doctor and was adamant that he was able to take care of himself. His health deteriorated until he developed a persistent and troubling cough. I would listen to his groaning at nights and his cough between his troubled sleep, especially when he woke up to use the bathroom. Finally one night, I awoke suddenly, feeling very troubled. My home felt as if there was a black shadow of death hanging over the house. I could not shake the feeling and immediately asked my friend and associate pastor who is a nurse to impress on my brother that he must get to the closest hospital. I knew she had a difficult assignment on her hands, but if anyone could get him to do that, it had to be her. The moment they arrived at the hospital, an expected phone call came. He was dying; every organ was failing rapidly. The doctors went to work, and before surgery, his heart failed three times. The church was immediately notified, and everyone from everywhere gathered at our facility, at my home, and at the hospital, and prayer was sent up round-the-clock. I was present when his heart stopped. I saw the monitors for myself, and almost without thinking, I grabbed every hand next to me and prayed until his heartbeat returned. Seconds seemed like eternity as we waited. For approximately two weeks, we waited as he was placed on life support after open-heart surgery. The doctors explained repeatedly that he was very sick and that we should expect the worse. We, nevertheless, kept praying. We were informed that the surgery was successful, but they were unable to reconnect both kidneys, so one kidney was left. The prognosis, at the best, was that he would remain on dialysis for the rest of his life. We kept praying for full recovery and saw a miracle happen right before our eyes. I was on my way to work as usual, driving down the Garden State Partway, while my brother was in a coma and on life support for more than a week. I heard the Holy Spirit clearly say that I should pray for a new kidney. I confess that was new to me since I have never given consideration to the idea of God giving someone a new kidney. It sounded strange and ridiculous, but I complied. Within three days, my brother woke up suddenly. All tests revealed that his heart was healthy; there was no need for dialysis, and he was discharged from the hospital. He recuperated and returned to living a normal life. Diabetes, as far as I know, was no longer an issue. This was one of the many near-death experiences we have witnessed, and our agreement in prayer has brought restoration and healing. There are countless other testimonies relating to my experiences on the job, at home, and at church where I witnessed mighty miracles as a result of prayer.

The Power of the Word

It is impossible for the enemy to win us when we live the Word of God. Many of us are able to memorize the Word of God, repeat the Word from memory, and even preach and teach the Word. The challenge for us is whether we are able to, in the face of fear, believe and practice the Word. We must put the word of God to work in our lives. Why? The word is God, represents

God, and is indeed the nature of God alive in our lives. It means logos in Greek and signifies the spoken work such as when God spoke in Genesis and said, "Let there be light." The word has the power to create as God creates; the word has the power to go to work on our behalf. Literally speaking and praying the promises of God on our lives, as written in the Scriptures, will break generational curses, destroy the yoke of the enemy, and release us into our place of promise. The children of God have tremendous authority through the Word of God because God will never permit his word to be voided. We are the righteousness of God made possible through the death and resurrection of Christ and must live our lives based on the right we have as God's chosen people. When Israel entered the promise land, every enemy that surrounded them was nervous and intimidated because of one reason only. They heard about the victories obtained by Israel brought about by the monotheistic god they served. The kings and their nations heard about the Hebrews' deliverance from slavery; they heard about the parting of the Red Sea and Jordan, the recent events of Jericho, and the defeat of Ai was fresh in their minds. The enemy knew that they were in for trouble when Israel entered their land. The nature and characteristic of the enemy has never changed. If you are a threat to him, he will initiate trouble first in order to get you to remain where you are. The history and longevity of the proven word of God must be utilized as an invaluable weapon. We must know who we are in Christ, and like the Israelites under the leadership of Joshua, we must dispossess the enemy. The strategies of our warfare, as seen, cannot be like those of the enemy. We cannot be underhanded and deceptive. We do not fight with violence, cheat, steal, live selfishly, and behave disrespectfully. We fight with the truth, with integrity, without compromising, and negotiate only when we are directed by the Holy Spirit. The battle is always the Lord's, and it is never by might nor by power but by the spirit of God that we overcome. We must resist the enemy, and he will flee, and pray not to be led into temptation but rather that God will deliver us from evil. Our guiding principle is to live by the fruit of the Spirit as declared in Galatians 5: 22 "But the fruit of the Spirit is love, joy, peace, longsuffering, gentleness, goodness, faith" (KJV).

Power Points of This Chapter

- God specializes in taking people from obscurity to a place of prominence.
- Prayer is giving God permission to act on earth on our behalf.
- Prayer brings us closer to God; it takes us into the presence of God, builds intimacy with God, and thereby minimizes the significance of the problems we encounter.
- Speaking and praying the word of God on our lives as written in the Scriptures will break generational curses, destroy the yoke of the enemy, and release us into our place of promise.

Leaving a Legacy of Excellence

> I have fought a good fight, I have finished my course, I have kept the faith: Henceforth there is laid up for me a crown of righteousness.
>
> Timothy 4:7 (KJV)

"Leaving a legacy of excellence" is my personal motto, especially since I turned fifty. I know that I am living in my place of promise, and as a result, I am determined to give back in one capacity or another. It is my time to do succession planning. It is my time to mentor. It is my time to coach. It is my time to invest in lives. My goal now is to empower people by utilizing my time, experience, knowledge, and any resource I have to push people into their place of promise. Our goal must be to become more popular in death than in life. Every world changer, with Christ at the top of the list, became more famous in death than in life. Martin Luther King, Mahatma Gandhi, Mother Theresa, and countless others died for a cause. They had holy discontents and lived their lives to address a particular problem that resonated. They committed themselves completely to fight the ravages created by the problem they addressed. We who have been delivered from Egypt, have been fortunate to survive the journey, and have entered into our place of promise must give back something to change our world. Unquestionably, we see that our societies and indeed the world is on a path to destroy itself with poverty, diseases, disparities of all kinds, slavery, abortion, genocide, child labor, and a host of other anomalies. The traditional family is on the path of extinction, and we are forced directly and indirectly to accept and encourage nontraditional lifestyles that are in conflict with the Scriptures. We have a responsibility individually and collectively to become discontented with certain issues in order to save one life at a time. We are living in the best of times and in the worst of times. While we are surrounded by much evil and injustice, we are blessed with tools that can be utilized to fight back the forces of darkness that is invading our homes, schools, and the marketplace. I am confident that if the people of God become mobilized to make a difference, we can make significant inroads in changing our world.

Change Begins in Our Hearts

Transformation begins in the heart. We can change our world one person at a time. The mission begins with each individual accepting that we have a responsibility to ourselves, our family, and our community. Empowerment begins with the acquisition of knowledge, the kind of knowledge that is based on a strong foundation of good moral values, spiritual standards, and the Word of God. There are countless people who still believe that there is a god and that he holds us to high standards. It has been proven throughout history that any civilization without guiding principles will not last. The Word of God must become our compass and the tool that we utilize to transform our lives. It is impossible for a slave to free another slave. The concept is if we are liberated spiritually and are driven by purpose, we can begin to teach those around us and lead by examples. We should refrain from verbalizing everything but become proactive in living as good examples so that others will see us as their mentor.

Change Is Filtered in the Home

My goal in my home is to teach through my lifestyle. My daughters hear and see me pray. They see me practice good stewardship. They are cognizant of the standards I set in decision making, and they see integrity at work. I balance my responsibilities at home with church, secular job, and play and do not expect things from them that I do not first demonstrate. Sometimes, they express that as young people, it is difficult to keep up with my "impossible standards." The humor is I have never sat them down and explained what my standards are; I simply live them. Of the five who are married and moved out to start their own families, everyone, so far, returned to say thanks for teaching them how to cook, clean, do chores, pay the bills, pray, and more than anything else, to love God first. Several of them have given birth to children and are perpetuating the same lifestyle of excellence. We are by no means wealthy, or famous. We struggle with the same challenges of regular, normal people, but we have something far greater than fame and money. We have family, great friends, and valuable people in our lives. One simple act of permitting a few individuals to share my personal space and my heart has given birth to a generation that will carry on the same values indefinitely.

We must endeavor to surrender our lives to be trained and taught by the Holy Spirit in order to become disciplined. We do not have to follow the majority. The popular opinion is not always the right opinion. In fact, the truth is generally upheld by the minority in most cases. We must examine our lives objectively and where we find deficiencies, change those areas. The standards must be set first in our homes. Notice Israel, as a nation, has endured hardship and persecution probably more than any other race on earth. Yet they survived to tell their stories. They were never assimilated into other cultures to the point where they lost themselves, but the teachings remained in their homes, and the foundation was built upon strong family values grounded in their relationship with God. Each parent must take their responsibility in the home seriously as this is the place where character is molded. The role of the father and husband as head of the household must be maintained. Fathers must understand their responsibility and must not abdicate them but rather take the lead in spiritual matters as well as in maintaining harmony in their homes. Where there are weaknesses on the part of the father and the wife has strength, both parents must work together for the benefit of the family. Couples must complement each other rather than work against each other. They are partners with a goal of empowering the family unit.

The single-parent household is now a reality in our culture, and unfortunately, to a great extent. It has contributed to serious problems in our society. On the contrary, I can testify that it is not impossible to uphold a spirit of excellence in this family unit. The single parent must take charge, become the authority by setting standards, create boundaries and guidelines, and not be afraid of confronting. Rather than rewarding bad behavior, we must be vigilant in changing bad behavior. Children are not parents and cannot make decision for parents. I have observed countless parents who compensate by giving their children more gadgets, unnecessary amount of clothing, sneakers, and the like only to lose them in the end. It is the time that we spend together as a family that matters most; it is the example that we set, the words we speak, and the system of accountability and integrity that we build that will keep our children on the straight and narrow. My daughter was ridiculed in school by her peers, intimidated because she chose not to fight, cuss, smoke, and act like the majority. It was difficult at first, but at her graduation, she received scholarships and rewards despite the academic deficiencies and challenges, which were beyond her control. She easily found a job after graduation and entered college to begin a life that would take her into her destiny. Every good or bad behavior begins in the home, taken into the church, school, marketplace, and other institutions, after which they are used to shape our communities.

Making a Difference: Serving the Community

Families make up our communities, and as previously mentioned, character building begins at home. Parents blame the system, teachers, pastors, and the streets for the deterioration of values in our society when in fact it begins at home. Values then must be taken into our jobs every day in order to impact the people we spend most of our waking hours with. It is in the marketplace, the political institutions, the educational institutions, churches, entertainment centers—places where powerful and impactful decisions are made every day—that we must exercise our greatest influence. Our votes count. Our voices matter. Our relationships are significant. Our decision making abilities are paramount to changing our cultures. The war against destructive systems is great but not impossible to win; we must keep fighting to make a difference in every sphere of influence. We must take the principles taught in the home to our church which, for me, is the hope of our community and the world. I am at war, one that is being fought with the goal to return honor, dignity, and significance to the local church in the community. The church must be the hub of the community and must take the lead in maintaining principle, character, and good values. God's word clearly teaches that the place where good values are initiated is in the home. For how can we manage the church when our homes are in disarray? Churches should not only be a place where the doors are open on Sunday mornings for attendees to be entertained and to listen to a well-constructed sermon or speech. It must be a group of people and a facility offering more than the latter, challenging and engaging people's spirit, mind, and soul to take on the responsibility of the great command. We must be fired up to go on Monday, to change someone somewhere in a broken and lost world. Every sermon/message must be an assignment to help someone to move from Egypt to their place of promise. We must be vigilant in teaching the following in order to leave a legacy:

- Spiritual maturity
- Prioritizing by placing God first
- Valuing family, friends, and people everywhere
- Living for others, finding a cause, developing a holy discontent
- Practicing what you preach
- Encouraging and supporting learning
- Sharing one's resources: time, talent, and treasure

In leaving a legacy, we must identify the areas where the greatest difference can be made in our community. We will never be everything to all people, but we must be something to some people. My desire is to develop programs, initiatives, and collaborative systems that will benefit our youth. Our young people are the leaders of tomorrow and are desperately in need of guidance, encouragement, support, and understanding. They are faced with a gamut of new and strange circumstances that the preceding generations are completely unfamiliar with. I believe that the pace of technology has revolutionized our behavior, habits, family relationships, office relationships, etc., and the group that is most affected is the youth. Our children do not need to speak to others to be entertained; they do not need to ask questions to be educated. To a great extent, they are being molded by an invisible system that enters into their lives through television, telephone, smart phones, electronic games, gadgets, and more. They are becoming more and more isolated from positive influences of people, including their parents. We have a crisis on our hands and must reinvent our thinking and strategies in order to deal effectively with this social dilemma. Social media, for instance, is able to begin political upheavals and can create momentums that can ricochet across nations, cultures, and the world. The world is now a small place because of technology. Technological systems are able to unite young people across the world in an instant, and all at the same time, it is able to disrupt rather than create harmony. How can we harness this new knowledge to change the lives of our young people for the better? Rather than becoming intimidated and frightened, there are times when the weapons that are meant to destroy us can be turned around to create a greater good. It is now more critical than ever for us to join together and hang out in the world of our young people by becoming even more acquainted with their systems. We must seek to find a few good leaders from this generation, train them, teach them, and equip and release them into their world to make a difference. We cannot become indifferent to their world; rather, we must share their world by participating and understanding. For many, night has become day and day has become night. They prefer the flexibility of working at night and sleeping during the day whenever their schedule permits. Technology does not go to sleep, and they too do not seem to go to sleep. They are curious, impatient, and very visual, and most things must be accomplished speedily. All of these demand new methods of communication and interaction in order for us to change our communities.

Serving the Family

My goal is to foster the development of community empowerment centers that are affiliated with a local church. The dream is to create a nonthreatening environment where church meets the community. This model will involve volunteers as well as paid staff including young people who will invest their creative skills and talents with the goal to empower people. If you recall, Israel was expected to become the influence to the surrounding nations, not the reverse. They were expected by God to bring their religion into the promise land where the surviving surrounding nations would come to know the one true God. Community centers owned by churches will impact in the following manner:

- Provide family counseling
- Provide job training for undereducated families
- Provide after school extracurricular activities
- Provide general education programs
- Provide free meeting room space for community meetings
- Provide health fairs and college fairs
- Provide food and medicinal supplies for those in need

This model community center must be built on a foundation of prayer. At its core, there must be a prayer center or dedicated space that is set aside where people of any age along with their families can join hands in prayer for the success of all godly initiatives. My desire is to see us pray every day in an assigned location with the goal to seek radical change. Prayer teams with the same interests must plan strategically to pray in unity for change in our families and communities. My hope is that we will not stop praying until we see permanent public change in our community. I have witnessed the transformational power of God operating in Ossining, New York. At the start of our ministry, the community was plagued with drug dealers on the main street. There was an infestation of associated problems such as drug addiction, alcoholism, teenage pregnancies, and lack of education among the working poor and sexual immorality and violence among the youth. We prayed for changes in these areas both in homes and at our small rented space where we met for Bible studies. Finally, after about two years, we saw noticeable changes. The majority of the drug dealers relocated, and several young people who were deeply involved accepted Christ as their savior. Today, our church is noted for the high standard of education among its members. Everyone seems to automatically return to school the moment they become a member. Satan's desire is to keep the church within the four walls. His desire is to keep us thinking small, living small, and contributing small. His desire is to keep us in Egypt, locked in the chains of our past rather than living in a wealthy place.

God wants us to reach the world; what better way to accomplish this than to serve the families in our community. We have the power to change our community one family at a time.

Governor, Priest, and People

Recently, I addressed students and teachers at my Bible school and seminary. I was asked to speak from Haggai 2. The theme was "There Will Be Glory After This." My presentation surrounded the rebuilding of the temple by the governor of Jerusalem, the high priest, and the people. I emphasized that God spoke to three categories of people, encouraged them to be strong, and commanded them to work. Three questions were asked: Who is left among you that saw this house in its first glory? How do you see it now? Do you perceive it to be nothing in your eyes? In other words, let's reflect on the past and compare it with the present. God knew the answer, but he was making a point. The word "strong" in Hebrew, as used in this scripture, is Amats, which means to be alert physically and mentally, be encouraged, to confirm, to be steadfastly minded, establish, fortify, harden, increase, and prevail. The Hebrew word for work, as used here, is Melachah. This means all forms of human productivity. This was not a haphazard collection of activities and does not necessarily represent physical exertion; rather, the principle behind them is that they represent constructive, creative effort demonstrating man's mastery over nature.

The lesson in this story is that spiritual abilities must be merged with the political administration and the crafts in order for the work to be completed. All three categories of people from the community working together will accomplish the work. From a personal perspective, we cannot all be spiritual to accomplish God's work. Faith must work along with our plans and our creative abilities to ensure success. We must utilize our practical skills, administrative skills, leadership skills, and creative skills. The youth is generally more creative, while the older people are more well-trained in the crafts. We must have an amalgamation of all people in the community in order to see transformation. At times, we may need to call upon others—the decision maker, the intercessors, those who speak the language of the town's politician, or the contractor, carpenter, and even the electrician—but we must work together. Notice that included in the prophetic word is encouragement and admonition. The people were told to work. What is the significance of this? I believe God's intention was to keep them focused. It is critical that while we wait to be with our Lord in heaven, we occupy until he comes. Work keeps people occupied mentally, physically, and emotionally, especially when the resources are just not available to buy or build the best.

Hard Work Is Necessary

Constant hard work will pay off in the long run. At times, hard work does not necessarily bring us into our God-ordained destiny. Let's clarify, hard work that accompanies God's ordained goals and objectives will be completed successfully. Sometimes, we work hard and do not succeed because we work selfishly. God never wants his people to relax and wait because he made a promise that he would come in the future. Let's recall that God approached Moses at his work site and recruited him to go back to Egypt to bring God's chosen people out of bondage. I agree with Os Hillman when he stated, "Notice that God came to Moses's place of work during his workday-his work as a shepherd in the fields. Why is this ground holy? Because God's presence was there. That is the first lesson for all of us. Our work becomes holy when the presence of God resides there." In my lifetime, I have heard people say, "I am not going to college, neither will I invest in a house because the rapture may come at any time." While the rapture is imminent, it does not mean that we should not work to bring God's kingdom to earth. It's time for the church to influence our educational and economic systems. It's time for the church to influence family and culture. It's time for the church to influence the political system. Work denotes influence, and actively engaging our culture through work will make our voices resonate in the marketplace. Millions will never enter the doors of the church, so we carry a responsibility to touch the lives we encounter in the marketplace. Bottom line is everyone must be strong and work together to transform our world one community at a time.

Power Points of This Chapter

- Our goal must be to become more popular in death than in life. Every world changer, with Christ at the top of the list, became more famous in death than in life.

- Anyone who desires to be successful must first become humble and learn to submit to the small and the great.
- Getting to our place of promise prematurely can become self-destructive.
- Lack of experience and training that can only be gathered by years of learning life lessons can be a detriment rather than a benefit. It is of vital importance that we understand that God works in our lives from eternity, and it manifests in our time.
- The stops along the way teach great lessons that we are able to utilize later as they are needed. In fact, timing is a law all by itself. If we disrupt the timing of God for our lives by consistently taking matters into our hands, then we will for sure suffer the consequences of our immature behavior.
- Remember there is a price for success, and there is a cost for the call of God upon our lives

Enjoy the Journey!

> Nehemiah said, "Go your way, eat the fat, and drink the sweet, and send portions unto them for whom nothing is prepared: for this day is holy unto our Lord: neither be ye sorry; for the joy of the Lord is your strength."
>
> Nehemiah 8:10 (KJV)

My spiritual father once told me during a major painful transition period in my life to "enjoy the journey. Life is really not about the destination, it's about enjoying today because when you get there, it's not all that." From that day until now, that has been my guiding principle. I have made a decision that I will wake up every day to enjoy the day ahead. There are several important points I would like to make in this concluding chapter. Point number one is as long as you are alive, there will be a parallel of good times and bad times. We must position ourselves to accept the things we have no control over and trust our creator to move us from one point to another. Those things that we have the power to change, we work to change. We cannot be lackadaisical and complacent concerning the things that confront us. We must strive to be proactive at all times. I oftentimes encourage my children to seek for the passion and the drive to accomplish. I presented the subject of drive versus passion regarding accomplishing our goals to a mixed crowd. The main point of the subject was that we all must learn to enjoy the process as we work on assignments, projects, or goal-oriented activities. There are some of us who fail in the middle of every project, and then there is the other extreme where we cannot be satisfied. The more we accomplish, greater desire is generated to accomplish even more. If we are not careful, we will never stop to celebrate our successes. We must create a balance in terms of the way we conduct our lives. As we seek to reach our goals, we must engage our passion by connecting what we do in a healthy way so that we can enjoy the tasks that come with the process. On the other hand, we need to step back from our emotional state sometimes and seek to get the job done with the drive we have to achieve. We will never be passionate about everything we do neither will we have the drive in all instances. Some of the things that are important to our very survival are boring and uninteresting. It is our commitment to the goal that will get the job done. So whether we are bored or excited about where we are in the journey, we must always endeavor to look beyond our feelings and make a decision to stop for a moment and enjoy the journey.

The second point is that opportunities are oftentimes packaged as problems. We must endeavor to learn from the problems we face, utilize them as bridges that will get us into a new place, and learn from those incidences that we label as failures. On occasions, the seemingly negative situations that confront us are, more times than not, learning experiences. Our situations and circumstances do not have to control our lives. We must live to take control of every moment rather than running ourselves wreck on the tidal wave of negative emotions that accompany the problems we are faced with. I have matured over the years not because of the fun times and the good things that happen, but rather, it was those highly challenging problems that taught me major life skills.

- I learned to budget when there were serious financial constraints in my life.
- I learned to write business letters and plans when I was forced to purchase real estate and could not afford to pay professionals for everything.
- I learned leadership skills when there were few staffs to accomplish the great variety of jobs in the organizations I managed.
- I learned public speaking when I was challenged to stand before municipal councils, zoning boards, and professional groups because of lack of resources.
- I learned integrity, dedication, and commitment to relationships because I endured the pain of abandonment and rejection.
- I learned to make a difference because I was hurt by selfish people in my life.

Every one of us is able to learn from our mistakes as well as from pain inflicted upon us by other people. Every moment can be a time of learning. We do not have to see the worst in everything because the fact is all things work together for the good of those who love the Lord and are called according to his purpose. The arrows that were meant to destroy you can be your vehicle to your destination. The things we sow, we end up reaping, and life seems to be a circle. As they say, what goes around comes around. Our good deeds will eventually catch up with us. When we get to our destiny, we should not live in regret because we did not make full opportunity of the chances that came our way when negative situations arise. The friendships we lose along the way will give birth to new friends at a later point in our lives. I have seen people come and go in my life. It appears that those who do not remain were not meant to remain. Sometimes, people are our greatest detriment to success, yet they could also be our greatest asset. Many of my high school and college friends are simply memories of a previous chapter in my life. Oftentimes I meet old friends and try to rekindle relationships, but for one reason or another, they seem to work out very frequently. Sometimes, all that we need are memories of relationships because as we mature, we do outgrow people and some types of relationships. It appears that there are seasons in our lives, and each season gives birth to a new set of people who are meant to be either to humble us or to perfect us. We must take note that the things that are lasting and fulfilling are sometimes the things we take for granted, such as faith, friends, and family.

Now Is Your Time

This popular cliché resonates true for me and should for you as the reader. It has great meaning for me personally because approximately ten years ago, I asked one of my colleagues to conduct a research at the library on the word we currently use as a popular name for our church. A few days after the request, the librarian came back to me and announced, "I have good news." The word means "now is your time." I knew then that the word I saw in my dream was information from God to me. Subsequent to that date, I frequently remind myself and those who I encourage through public speaking, counseling, and regular conversations that their time is now. Now means today. It means this moment, or this chapter, or season in your life. It further denotes our life as we live it and experience it. Your time means your moment, your opportunities, and your journey. You were given only one chance at life by the Almighty God. As previously mentioned, you cannot afford to destroy the only chance you have to accomplish your dreams. You must arise, think positively, believe in yourself in a healthy way, love yourself in a healthy way, and understand that you are loved by God. Knowing these things gives you the right to claim your God-given inheritance on this planet. You are not mediocre, simple, frail, and lost. You have gifts, attributes, talents, and resources that you can use effectively to transform our world. You must seek to change yourself in a positive way, and while you do that, you will impact your family, friends, and colleagues in a positive way.

My greatest joy is to see the people around me happy. I aim to see peace and order around me. I consider myself successful when those whom I lead are successful. So I encourage people every day to keep trying, look toward tomorrow with hope, and constantly put plans in place to make things that we dream about happen. It amazes me how many of us go about our business, relying on the opinions of others from day to day when we could have put our own plans in place to make things happen for us. Success breeds success, and similarly, failure breeds failure. It is critical that we take the small successes and build upon them to create greater things. We do not have to begin at the top. What is most important is that we start somewhere and keep moving. When it's your time, you must live out your own God-given dreams. Do you notice that great people enjoy having people around them to serve their needs but in the process may not necessarily care about the dreams of their subordinates? They will go to any length to ensure that they are served without realizing that we are here to serve others. Few great leaders become mentors in the long run. If there is no role model or mentor in your life, you can pursue a godly path with direction from the Word of God. Follow those biblical characters who paved the way, endured hardship, but nevertheless, reached their destination. None of the people I know who have made it are perfect. They are all folks with negative past experiences, faults, and failures. They have a common thread in their DNA. They all simply decided to get up and move on with their lives. We cannot run away from ourselves and our personalities. Some people I know are quick to make major decisions, such as relocating, ending relationships, and quitting whenever they encounter crisis in their lives. What we must do is to face our fears and love ourselves as we are loved by God. We all can move on with our lives by taking the plunge into unknown waters. You will never know whether you are able to swim the waters of life until you dive in. Indecisiveness is worse than actually making a decision, which ends in failure.

Never resolve to blaming people for your mistakes. I hear that statement all the time in my world. People blame their parents, their siblings, their ex-wives, and ex-husbands for their failure. Some even go as far as to blame their heritage and culture for where they are and who they are. I consider those comments, when I hear them, as lame excuses. I have seen people rise from abject poverty, tremendous pain, vicissitudes to reach pinnacles in their career, and other personal goals. They do so because they take responsibility for their actions and decisions and understand that we never chose to be born in a particular race or in a specially selected place. Many people have more opportunities than others; however, we all can make use of what we have. Blaming others means that you will wait for others to make it happen for you. It is never the responsibility of the people in our lives to make us happy. We have a personal responsibility to take charge of our destinies and seek for corresponding opportunities that will move us from one point to another. Every day, we must look for moments when doors of opportunities are opened. Doors are not opened forever. We must learn to recognize when those moments arise. Sometimes, it takes one small decision to make major changes. Do not allow fear to stop you, but rather, face your fears with confidence. The things that appear most intimidating can be overcome if we only apply courage. Courage, for me, is having the ability to face our fears.

Learn to live your life creatively. There is a part of the creator that is embedded in every human being. If you believe that you do not have what we classify as creative gift, you refuse to harness your innate abilities to become successful. If you are not academically oriented, you can find and develop one of your skills, turn it into your vocation, and fulfill your dreams. Many of us are deficient in many ways, but everyone has a talent. There are some of us who are multi-talented, while others appear to have very few gifts. Identify what you are good at, and utilize your gifts to plan your goals. In other words, set your goals and objectives with your gifts as your foundation. Have you ever asked someone who knows you well to evaluate you based on what they see? You may be amazed that people may see abilities in us that we overlook.

Every day Is a Day of Thanksgiving

A spirit of gratitude is essential to your well-being. Giving thanks to God for the small things helps to build our character. A thankful spirit will renew our joy and appreciation for life. This demeanor will teach us that we should not take life for granted neither should we take the blessings we receive for granted. There is a cost for everything. Nothing is really free. Even the salvation we experience in Christ was paid for by the blood of Jesus, God's only son. It is important that we remember that there are always other people around us who have far less than what we have, whether intellectually, spiritually, or materially. People everywhere suffer from lack in one form or another. We will never have everything we desire and must be careful not to operate from a greedy point of view. I believe that once we appreciate the small things and take care of them respectfully, we will graduate to receive greater things and responsibilities. In one of the parables Jesus taught, the master replied, "Well done, good and faithful servant! You have been faithful with a few things. I will put you in charge of many things. Come and share your master's happiness!" Learn to say thank you to everyone who does a kind act on your behalf. People will do more when you show them appreciation. In fact, one of the greatest motivator to an individual is to show them that what they do matters. This is true in the family, home, and work environment. People, in general, are encouraged to serve when they are appreciated. Children even will improve in their level of confidence when they know that their opinion, input, and work is valued. We build solid relationships when we plan moments of acknowledgements just to say thanks to those who encourage, participate, cheer us on, mentor us, coach us, and the like. Some people in our lives may not necessarily give their comments and opinions, but they simply smile or nod their affirmation. Never take people for granted, but let them know directly or indirectly that they matter. I serve in many capacities as a leader where I sometimes feel embarrassed to take credit for great accomplishments because I may envision the project. It is the people who surround me who bring their diverse skills, gifts, and attributes to the table that really make it happen. Life is essentially a network of people, circumstances, and situations coming together. None of us would be where we are today without people in our lives. So let's give thanks for the small things as well as the large things.

The Joy of the Lord Is Your Strength

Energize your life with the joy of the Lord as your strength. On countless occasions, I feel like just lying down in my bed on a rainy morning and go back to sleep. This happens frequently during the winter months, especially whenever there is snow and ice on the outside. Who wants to face the day when there is bad weather, particularly when you live a long drive from the office? This surely resonates for all of us. Any life that is lived based on personal feelings will end in failure. Feelings of laziness, lethargy, sleepiness, lack of motivation, and emotional distress affect all of us as humans. We, however, cannot allow negative feelings to control our lives. These enemies within us will control our mobility, prevent us from achieving, and stop us from moving from one place to another. There are times when we must fight harder than other times to overcome them and move on. These bad feelings breed procrastination, allow us to waste valuable time, and miss moments in our lives when we could have gone much further.

You must have heard the saying that joy is completely different from happiness. The word "happiness" is oftentimes defined based on its relationship or ties with material stuff. Most people feel cheerful when they receive good news, accomplish a goal, receive money, or other material stuff. There is some consensus that good feelings based on the latter things will not last. As time lapses and the good feelings wear off, the person becomes sad. Joy, on the other hand, is also a good feeling but is not necessarily tied or related to those things that engender happiness. There is an abundance of Bible stories and scriptural references that proves that having the presence of God in our lives provides joy. The Holy Spirit, for those who are not aware, is not simply an influence but a person. This means there is a presence of intellect, emotion, and will. Consequently, those who rely on the support of the Holy Spirit in their lives will notice that he teaches, guides, testifies, convicts, regenerates, intercedes, etc. Those who are led by the Spirit, meaning that they surrender their lives to God daily, demonstrate the fruits of the spirit, which is love, joy, peace, long-suffering, gentleness, meekness, temperance, faith, and self-control. The moment the individual changes his lifestyle and accepts Jesus Christ as lord and savior of their lives, the most beautiful things happen. Freedom and a release from the tendency to be happy occurs. Joy replaces happiness, and the Holy Spirit provides the support necessary to maintain this position/state of joy. We can always look to the future knowing that tomorrow will always be better than today because my emotional state is not dependent on stuff, but rather, on having God in my life. I have joy because I am free.

Think Big: Maintain the Right Attitude

Your thought life is important and has significance to the journey. Wherever you are right now, whether at the Red Sea, Sinai, or Jordan, never allow your thoughts to be controlled by negative forces. In addition, never think small. I previously shared how my spiritual father told me to think big, and from that day onwards, my world changed. I no longer look to get little things from life, but I changed my perspective. It has been proven by psychologists and other medical personnel that positive thinking is essential for success. Our bodies respond to messages that are sent from our minds. Everyone lives out their thought life in reality. If you think that you cannot succeed, that is exactly how it will play out in your life later. As you recall the life of the Hebrews, they were out of Egypt, but to a great extent, they continued to think like slaves. They were not proactive, positive, or independent thinkers. They had the greatest mind in the universe, their God, but were not successful in submitting to receive the thinking of God. Notice the way God thought for them. The plan was to remove them from a small place where they did not own property, had no rights to make their own decisions, and to take them into the promise land.

The promise land represents a much larger place. Awaiting them was the right to own their own place/land. Awaiting them was the privilege to have any amount of children they chose. Awaiting them was the right to institute their own government. Awaiting them was the opportunity to plant and grow their own food in any quantity. Bottom line is freedom follows slavery. Small thinking equates slavery; big thinking equates a greater level of freedom. God wants the best for us because he owns the best. Slavery, poverty, lack, and sickness were never created for you and me. These things were brought into our world because of the disobedience of man. We look ultimately for a new earth and new heavens. While we are here, we must hope for the best, work for the best, and seek to develop a spirit of excellence in all facets of our lives.

Appendix

Points to Remember

- Most people, by nature, judge their future based on their past. Your future cannot be seen from your past experiences or your present circumstances. Your future must be seen from your place of promise.
- The devil's desire is to keep you in Egypt, a place of sin and bondage. God's desire is to liberate you and take you on a journey with him to your final destination. God will move you from glory to glory.
- Maintaining the right perspective during difficult times is paramount to your future success. We must maximize the moment rather than complain and grumble about it.
- God will always win in the long run. Your future will always look brighter than the present because God's ultimate plan for us will be accomplished when we reign with him in heaven or in the millennial kingdom.
- History is our foundation and, to a great extent, can be used to mold the future, but it should never be used to stop our dreams.
- Use your stops along the way to build character and integrity out of humility and obedience.

- Find a secret place in God to build intimacy. To replenish for the journey is meant to bring you closer to your maker.
- While you use faith, develop a plan, remain focused, think positively, and see your destiny through the eyes of God.
- Pray without ceasing, pray until something happens, and pray after it happens.
- God is going to make you laugh. Utilize the weapon of laughter to encourage yourself during difficult times.
- Never sweat the small stuff. Think big on whatsoever things are honest, whatsoever things are right, whatsoever things are pure, whatsoever things are lovely, and whatsoever things are of good report, if there is any virtue and if there is any praise think on these things.
- Take the lead and take the risk with God; life is an adventure with all kinds of possibilities waiting to be explored. The life of faith is inherently a life of risk.
- Live to leave a legacy. It's never about you; it's always about others.
- Develop a holy discontent, intercede for a solution, put a plan in place, and engage people to bring your plan to accomplishment.
- Never take people for granted, including your enemies.
- God loves you. He has a plan for your life. He wants to use you for his glory.

About the Author

Dr. Joan E. Whittaker is a visionary, entrepreneur, leader, and role model. She is often described as a world changer because of the positive impact she has had on individuals and the community.

Ms. Whittaker was born in Jamaica, West Indies, and immigrated to the United States in 1988 in order to attend graduate school. After twelve months, she graduated with a master's degree in library and information science and has served in her profession since then in one capacity or another.

During the last fourteen years, Joan E. Whittaker has served in Irvington Public Library; first as the director of children's services for five years, then as the library director for the past nine years.

Since being appointed director of the library, Dr. Whittaker has revitalized the services and programs of the library and has transformed the library from its traditional role to the hub of the town. Dr. Whittaker refurbished the adult library in 2000 for the very first time since the library was built in 1968. She later tackled the children's room and office areas. Today, the library is a bright inviting place and attracts over 20,000 visitors per month.

Joan E. Whittaker has been proactive in providing cutting-edge technology to the people who use the library. In 2000, she designed a state-of-the-art computer lab and completed the project within three months. Several grants were written and funds were received to purchase computers. Recently, the Bill and Melinda Gates Foundation Grants completely furnished the lab with eleven computers. Two other computer centers were built in recent years to meet the demand for public access computers. A variety of free computer classes are offered almost every day of the week to anyone from anywhere.

The new mission of the library is to be the cultural and educational resource center for the residents of the township of Irvington and its neighboring communities. In addition to free computer classes, there is an adult literacy program, a book-of-the-month club, a poets corner, monthly art exhibits, summer youth reading book fest, cultural diversity appreciation events, business and legal services, teen advisory council, dance ensembles, and a variety of daily children's programs.

Joan E. Whittaker's ability, knowledge, enthusiasm, creativity, and proactive stance as a leader resulted in her becoming a productive and outstanding director in the township of Irvington.

Joan E. Whittaker has chosen to advance her horizons in recent years by relocating from New Jersey to Ossining, New York, where she is founder and senior pastor of the House of Refuge Community Church, a.k.a. HORAC Ministries. Her leadership skills have impacted thousands as she touches the lives of many through her dynamic and moving public speaking. She is unquestionably a role model, particularly for teenagers, as evidenced in the membership of the church where over seventy percent of the members are young people.

Today, Joan E. Whittaker spends her daytime hours managing Irvington Public Library as well as serving on several community boards; and her evenings, nights, and weekends as the pastor of the House of Refuge Community Church in Ossining, New York.

Notes

When God Changes Direction

Monroe, Miles, *The Glory of Living: Keys to Releasing Your Personal Glory*, Merrimac, Massachusetts: Destiny Image Publishers, 2005.

Warren, Rick, *Purpose Driven Life*, Grand Rapids, Michigan: Zondervan, 2002.

Celebrate Your Victories

Hillman, Os, Change Agent: Engaging Your Passion to Be the One Who Makes a Difference, Florida: Charisma House, 2011

Rephidim: A Place of Refreshing

Jakes, T.D., *Reposition Yourself: Living Life without Limits*, New York: Atria Books, 2007.

Let's Go to Mount Sinai

Bevere, John, *The Fear of the Lord: Discover the key to Intimately Knowing God*, Lake Mary, Florida: Charisma House, 1997

Taking Territories

Hillman, Os, *Change Agent: Engaging Your Passion to Be the One Who Makes a Difference*, Florida: Charisma House, 2011

Maxwell, John, *Maxwell Study Bible*, Nashville, Tennessee: Thomas Nelson, 2007

Dealing with the Enemy

Trimm, Cindy, *The Art of War for Spiritual Battle: Essential Tactics and Srategies for Spiritual Warfare*, Lake Mary, Florida: Charisma House, 2010

Leaving a Legacy of Excellence

Hillman, Os, Os, *Change Agent: Engaging Your Passion to Be the One Who Makes a Difference*, Florida: Charisma House, 2011

732 215 6205 (DOD)
Rahway NJ

732 163 5350 Neeraj Krushik
     7